Winning Stitches

HAND QUILTING SECRETS  50 FABULOUS DESIGNS  QUILTS TO MAKE

Elsie M. Campbell

C&T PUBLISHING

Text © 2004, Elsie M. Campbell
Artwork © 2004 C&T Publishing, Inc.

Publisher: Amy Marson
Editorial Director: Gailen Runge
Editor: Ellen Pahl
Technical Editor: Katrina Lamken, Joyce Engels Lytle
Copyeditor: Diane Kennedy-Jackson
Proofreader: Stacy Chamness
Cover Designer: Christina D. Jarumay
Book Designer: Dawn DeVries Sokol
Design Director: Diane Pedersen
Illustrator: Richard Sheppard
Production Assistant: Jeff Carrillo
Quilt Photography: Sharon Risedorph
Digital Photography: Diane Pedersen
Published by C&T Publishing, Inc., P.O. Box 1456, Lafayette, California, 94549

Front cover: *Star Flower* by Elsie M. Campbell
Back cover: *Trapunto Mini* by Elsie M. Campbell

Permission has graciously been given by Carol Doak to allow us to show a photo of the **Little Amish Flower Garden** quilt made from a pattern in her book, *Easy Machine Paper Piecing*, 1994.

Library of Congress Cataloging-in-Publication Data

Campbell, Elsie.
  Winning stitches : hand quilting secrets, 50 fabulous designs, quilts
to make / Elsie M. Campbell.
       p. cm.
Includes bibliographical references and index.
  ISBN 1-57120-225-0 (trade paper)
  1. Quilting—Patterns. I. Title.
  TT835.C3568 2004
  746.46—dc22

                          2003017019

Printed in China
10 9 8 7 6 5 4 3 2 1

Contents

Dedication

This book is dedicated to the memory of my mother, Ella May Goebel Reusser, who first put a needle in my hands. She encouraged all my creative endeavors and was my biggest fan. Also to the earlier generations of quilters in both my family and my husband Ken's family, including my grandmothers, Katherine Fast Goebel, Martha Krehbiel Reusser, and Ken's grandmothers, Laura Cayot Kassik, Ruth Williams Campbell, and to our respective great-grandmothers, Anna Risser Goebel and Alice Cayot for making many inspirational quilts.

Ella May Goebel Reusser—1921–2002

Acknowledgments

Family and friends enrich every person's life. I have been particularly blessed with many special people in mind.

First, thanks go to Ken Campbell, my patient and supportive husband, who has encouraged my endeavors through the years with his willingness to forego a clean house in favor of warm quilts on the beds, and to cook family meals when I was busy with project deadlines.

Second, my two sons, Kelly and Kerry, have enriched my life beyond words with their ideas, expert criticism, computer savvy, and talents in photography and art.

Third, I also want to thank the Deer Creek, Oklahoma, Mennonite Mission Society ladies for keeping a rich quilting heritage alive and well. These quiet, unassuming quilters provided by their living example, ideal role models. They support each other through difficult times, celebrate life's events together, and generously share both time and money to help others.

And last, but not least, I wish to thank friends from several wonderful quilt guilds from across the United States, including the Walnut Valley Quilter's Guild of Winfield, Kansas; Stitch 'n Time Guild of Elk Lake, Pennsylvania; Crazy Country Stitchers of Montrose, Pennsylvania; and Miss Kitty's Quilters of Dodge City, Kansas. Special thanks to Doll Yunker of Miss Kitty's for finishing one of the projects for this book when I ran out of time. These wonderful quilters have been instrumental to my career in many ways. From nursing me through shoulder surgery and sponsoring great guild (not guilt!) trips to numerous quilt shops, to inspirational Show and Tells at meetings, these special people have contributed many behind-the-scenes hours to help make this book a reality.

Introduction

I grew up with a needle in my hand—literally. My mother told me that as soon as I could walk and talk, whenever she would sit down to sew, I let her know that I wanted to sew, too. She would thread a needle and knot the ends together, then hand it to me along with a bit of cloth.

It wasn't long before I moved on to the sewing machine. Mom had an old treadle machine that Dad altered to run with an electric motor. When she disconnected the electric motor, my younger sister Linda and I were allowed to "sew." We were still preschoolers at the time, so our little legs were too short to operate the treadle! We soon devised our own method of stitching. Linda would turn the wheel while I sewed, then we would trade positions. Mom taught us how to trace around a cardboard square onto cloth, making sure that the squares touched, so as not to waste any fabric. We carefully cut out the pieces and stitched them into four-patch blocks. Years later, Mom found those old blocks made from our childhood clothing scraps, and by adding a multitude of plain alternate blocks and sashing, she was able to fashion two identical, bed-sized quilts from them, one for Linda and one for me. My husband and I still sleep under that quilt during the winter months.

The years that followed were busy ones. I attended college, married Ken, raised two sons, and taught public school. I made quilts for my children to use, but it wasn't until 1987 that I returned to quiltmaking for pleasure. In 1992, I began exhibiting quilts at national-level shows. It didn't take too many shows before I discovered that the judges liked my hand quilting. I decided to focus on this skill by constructing my quilts from solid color fabrics (busy prints tend to camouflage quilting stitches), with large, open areas for fancy quilting. My quilts soon started earning many awards and much recognition.

I particularly enjoy the meditative nature and portability of hand quilting. One of my unfinished quilts logged thousands of miles with me one summer, traveling to the Grand Canyon on vacation, to St. Louis for a church conference, and to Odessa, Texas, for a family visit. I stayed very happy in the back seat of the family van stitching the miles away. In the evenings, quilting was my reward for a long day teaching school. It gave me something to do while enjoying television with the family. If I had quilted my quilts by machine, I would have been isolated in my sewing room for hours on end. Thus, most of my designs, and those included in this book, were created for hand quilting. However, many can easily be adapted for continuous-line machine quilting, and I include some tips on how to do that in this book.

When you page through this book, in addition to the quilting designs, you'll find methods for marking, and basting, plus descriptions of tools and products that I have found to make hand quilting easier. Keep in mind that these are methods that work well for me. They are not necessarily the best techniques or the only methods that work—they are just my way of doing things. If you find them useful, adapt them to your unique situation. If you have other ways that work well for you, do things your tried-and-true way.

You'll find that you don't really need a lot of space or fancy equipment to audition, size-to-fit, mark, and hand quilt an heirloom quilt. All award-winning hand quilting takes is just a few simple pieces of equipment, like a hoop, needle and thread, and a little time to sit back, relax, and enjoy your journey through the world of quilting.

Happy stitching,

Elsie

Hand Quilting Up Close

You know it when you see it—a showstopper quilt. It's a fabulous quilt with marvelous color, stunning patterns, and wonderful quilting. The quilt calls to you and shouts, "Come closer! See what else I have to offer." As you approach the quilt, the pieced or appliquéd pattern draws you in even further, and up close, the quilting becomes apparent. Then, and only then, can you appreciate the quiltmaker's point of view as she spent time taking the stitches that completed the quilt.

The Judges' Point of View

Even though you may instinctively know good hand quilting when you see it, what characteristics do judges of large, national shows look for in outstanding hand quilting? Let's look at some of the questions that come up. (Please note that this is not a complete listing of all the points considered in judging quilts. These guidelines are specific to hand quilting.)

The first question that may come to mind is, "How many stitches are there per inch?" There is some debate about whether to count the stitches and spaces between the stitches or to count only the stitches that show on top. Most professional judges agree that only the stitches showing on the top are counted. If the stitches are relatively small, $\frac{1}{16}$" or less (8 stitches or more per inch), then other factors are considered in determining which quilting is best.

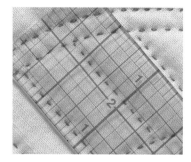

Detail of a quilt with a 1"-wide ruler laid next to the stitches.

Good hand quilting stitches are characterized by consistency and evenness. The space between the stitches should be the same length as the stitches. The stitches should be a consistent length over the entire quilt. Stitch length in the top border should be the same as the length of the quilting stitches in the center of the quilt and along the opposite side of the quilt.

Here are some additional questions judges may ask regarding the quilting and quilting stitches.

• **Does the quilting pattern enhance the overall effect of the quilt?** The quilting pattern should be appropriate for the style of the quilt. It may not be necessary to stitch intricate feathered scallops in the borders of a folk art quilt. Conversely, large, utility stitches would most certainly be out of place on a Baltimore Album or an elegant appliquéd quilt.

• **Does the quilting pattern fill the space and hold the layers of the quilt together?** While some battings may be quilted at 10" intervals, that is not adequate for a quilt that you want to last or display in a show. Even quilting every 3" to 4" is probably not enough to be considered for top awards in national-level competition.

• **Is the quilting evenly distributed across the quilt?** Underquilted areas will tend to sag when the quilt is hung. Areas that are quilted more densely than others will draw up and cause puckering.

• **Are straight lines straight and curves smooth and graceful?** Crosshatching lines should be perfectly straight, and evenly spaced. Feathers and other curved designs shouldn't have bumps, bulges, or points.

• **Are the stitches on the back as attractive as those on the front of the quilt?** The length of the stitches should be the same on the back as on the front.

• **Is the quilting thread chosen appropriate for hand quilting?** Hand quilting thread needs to be fine in gauge, smooth in texture, and strong enough to travel through the quilt layers many, many times without fraying or breaking.

• **Does the quilting thread color enhance the overall design?** Generally, color is a personal choice. However, if your quilt is a reproduction of an antique quilt, study the color of thread used in the original quilt. If you want to make an authentic-looking Amish-style quilt, use black or brown thread.

If you are a beginning hand quilter, choose a thread color that closely matches the background fabric of the quilt. The stitches will appear smaller and more even.

If you are an experienced hand quilter with excellent stitches, show them off by using a contrasting color thread. I like to stitch feathers or other figures in contrasting colors. I stitch background quilting in thread that matches the fabric.

• **Are the seams pressed flat and is the construction well executed?** At first glance, this may appear to be a construction issue rather than a quilting issue, but no matter how expertly a quilt is quilted, if it is poorly constructed, it will not be a contender for top awards.

Seams affect how easy the quilt is to quilt. Large, bulky seams that have pleats caused by incorrect pressing techniques are difficult if not impossible to quilt through by hand. Learn to stitch straight, even seams, and press seams properly to eliminate bulk.

I press most seams open in quilts that I intend to hand quilt for several reasons. First, seams should not shadow through the quilt top. When seams are pressed to one side, it is not always possible to press seam allowances toward the darker fabric; the darker seam must be trimmed slightly so it falls completely under the lighter seam allowance. Second, seam intersections where seams are pressed to one side can be too bulky to be easily hand quilted. By pressing seams open, extra layers of cloth are eliminated at those intersections.

• **Do quilting stitches flow flawlessly across heavy seams?** Quilting stitches should go through all three layers of the quilt and be as evenly spaced across seams as they are in other areas of the quilt.

The Quiltmaker's Point of View

As in nearly every other worthwhile creative endeavor, practice makes perfect! Entering quilts in competition gives you a chance to compare your work against a standard of excellence established by the judging staff. My experience is that, nearly always, judges are encouraging and not highly critical. Pay attention to their comments, do your research for ways to improve, and practice your art.

Study the positive things judges have to say. These are your strengths. If piecing is your forté, concentrate on making intricately pieced patterns. If appliqué brings the best compliments, make an exquisite, one-of-a-kind appliqué quilt. If hand quilting draws the judge's attention, incorporate large, unpieced areas into your quilt; choose solid fabrics for those parts where you can indulge in beautiful designs.

Next, focus on your weak areas. Read books on the subject. Ask questions of quiltmakers whose work you admire. Take classes and practice, practice, practice.

Make the effort to improve your skills with each new quilt you make. Even if you never exhibit your quilts in shows or find yourself in the winner's circle, the rewards for doing your best are many. Be proud of your accomplishments!

Fitting It All In

Envision this scenario: You've spent hours and hours researching antique and vintage quilts, looking through design books, and shopping for the perfect quilting pattern for your quilt. The idea for the best motif is taking shape in your mind. You've found a stencil that contains all the right design elements, but it isn't the right size or shape to fit the spaces on your quilt. Or you've found a pattern that fits, but it just doesn't have all the design elements you want. Frustration is the name of the "choosing-the-quilting-design" game for many novice quiltmakers and even for some of us who are more experienced.

Choosing a Quilting Design

If your quilt top is finished and you are ready to choose the quilting design, begin by answering a series of questions. Is the quilt pieced, appliquéd, or is it a combination of techniques? Is the design based on a traditional pattern or a contemporary adaptation? Is it an antique reproduction or does it contain folk art elements? What is the style of the quilt? Is it formal or informal?

Quilting designs should be compatible with the style of the quilt. An overall large and swirling free-form pattern may be appropriate for a contemporary style of quilt but this same pattern would most likely look out of place on a traditional Baltimore Album-style quilt. If your quilt resembles an antique or historical quilt, study examples in books and at quilt shows. How did other quiltmakers choose to quilt similar quilts? Do you like the motifs they used in their work? Make a few sketches or start looking for similar examples in stencils or pattern books.

Did you construct your quilt from many busy prints? If so, fancy quilting patterns won't show up

well, so stick with quick and simple in-the-ditch or outline quilting. Other good choices for scrappy quilts are overall patterns like Baptist fan or clamshells.

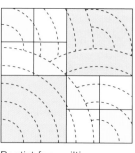
Baptist fan quilting

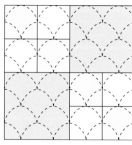
Clamshell quilting

How much time do you have to devote to the quilting process? Are you good at hand quilting? Do you enjoy doing it? In general, the more intricate and fancy the quilting pattern, the longer it will take to quilt.

Feather quilting

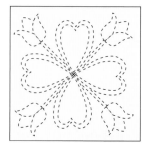
Motif quilting

Another consideration is how you intend for the quilt to be used. Wall quilts do not require heavy quilting and do not get heavy use, so you can pretty much quilt them as much as you want. A baby quilt will be laundered frequently, and the little owner will probably outgrow it as fast as he does his clothes. Quilting a baby quilt should be straightforward, simple, and quick to do. As a general rule, quilts that are going to be loved to death and laundered frequently do not justify the hundreds of hours you would spend hand quilting fancy feathers or other dense designs. Simple, quick patterns are better for quilts that are made to be used heavily.

If you haven't constructed your quilt top yet, consider including large, open areas for fancy quilting designs. Maybe you found a wonderful quilting design and are eager to use it in something. So who says you can't design your next quilt around the quilting design? That's exactly what I did with the quilt *Let Freedom Ring,* shown on page 50. I purposely made blocks the size I would need to showcase the designs.

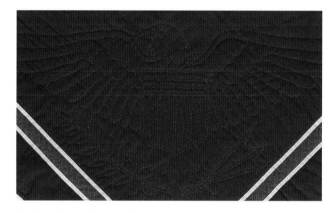

Let Freedom Ring detail

Let your own sense of design guide you when choosing quilting patterns. Select ones that you personally like, because after all, it's your quilt! If you're not confident of your choices, do some homework. Study quilt books and magazines, check out the stencils that your local quilt shop carries, or attend quilt shows. Take your camera along, if photographs are permitted. Carry a sketch pad and pencil with you everywhere you go because you never know when that "Aha!" moment will come. Clip magazine pages and keep them in a file along with your sketches. When you have a collection of ideas, go through them and see if there is a particular kind of pattern you are drawn to. Soon you will be able to pick and choose the perfect quilting patterns for your quilts.

Sizing Patterns to Fit

You've settled on a wonderful quilting design for your quilt, but if you are like me, you'll soon discover that it doesn't quite fill the area you'd planned to use it in. It just isn't the right size. Don't panic! Here are several creative ways I've found to solve this problem.

Photocopying

The quickest, easiest, and most-obvious solution is to take the motif or pattern to a copy center and have it enlarged or reduced to fit. To determine the enlargement or reduction percentage, first measure the block or other area in which you'd like the pattern to fit. Then measure the pattern's dimensions. Divide the block's measurement by that of the pattern. Turn this figure into a percentage by moving the decimal point two places to the right. This is the exact number to use on the copy machine for enlarging or reducing.

As an example, let's say that the quilting design you've chosen is 8" square but your block is 10" square. Divide the quilt's block size of 10" by the pattern size of 8". The answer is 1.25. After moving the decimal place over, that becomes 125%. You'll need to enlarge the 8" pattern by 125%. Conversely, if your quilting design is 10" square, and your block is 8" square, divide 8 by 10, and you will reduce the pattern at 80% to fit your block. If the copy machine only has round figures like 125%, 150%, etc., I suggest that you use the next smaller percentage. Remember to subtract ½" from the block size to allow for the seams and to avoid quilting through seam allowances.

Isolating and Repeating Motifs

Another technique that I like to use to fit designs to specific areas is to take a single motif from the design and experiment with it to make an interesting block pattern.

Isolate an interesting part of the pattern, then repeat it to fill in other parts of a block. This is a great way to make circular designs fill a square. Study this example. This feathered wreath features four hearts in the center. Isolate the heart motif and add one to each corner of the square.

Lengthen the leaf to fit the space.

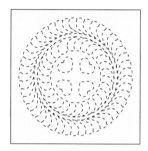 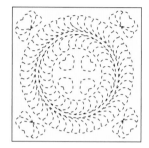

Simplifying

Simplifying designs is another way to reduce the size. Are there portions of the pattern that extend out from a central motif? Can some of them be deleted without losing the overall pleasing effect of the entire design? Some lines are simply not necessary to retain the essence of a motif, and others are. Experiment to see what works for the spaces and designs you have chosen.

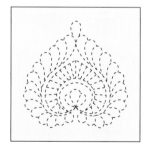 

Eliminate part of the design.

Sizing Border Patterns to Fit

Quilting designs used in borders can be made up of individual, separate motifs. Making sizing adjustments with these kinds of designs is easily done by simply allowing more or less space between individual motifs, elongating, or reducing the length of parts of the motifs. Patterns can be elongated or shortened by simply sliding the pattern back and forth as you trace the motif onto another sheet of paper.

One method I use for fitting quilting motifs into borders is to create or alter a pattern to fit the width of the border and the length of a single block of the quilt. You can reduce or enlarge with a copy machine, or add or delete motifs from the pattern. For example, if the blocks in the quilt are 8" square, and the border is 5" wide, find or alter a quilting motif to fit a 5" x 8" space. Then align each motif in the border with the seams between the blocks and design a turn to continue the flow of the quilting motif around the corner.

Align the motif with the block seams. Design a corner motif to connect the borders.

This method works well for both single borders and multiple borders. The corner turns will be longer for multiple borders and may or may not involve adding additional motifs.

The quilting design repeats in a border do not have to be the same length as the blocks in a quilt. Folding paper to the repeat length is another way to divide the border. This is a good method to use for rectangular quilts or quilts with different size blocks. Begin by cutting pieces of freezer paper the same size and shape as your borders. Do not include the corners in these pieces. Fold the paper border in half, then in quarters and maybe eighths for a large quilt. You can also fold the border into thirds and sixths, although this is a little harder to do.

Fold the paper in half, then in half again as many times as needed.

Or fold the paper in thirds.

Of course, you can always measure, and use math to make the border divisions, but I usually prefer the paper-folding technique to math. It's quick, and in some cases, more accurate. Once the paper is folded into repeats, you can alter the pattern, either reducing or enlarging it to fit, and add corners.

Marking the Quilt

I put quilting designs into three basic categories—ones that need no marking at all, those that are best marked as you stitch, and fancy quilting designs that are easiest to mark before layering and basting the quilt top, batting, and backing together.

No Marking Needed

Examples of designs that need no marking include quilting in-the-ditch, outline quilting, echo quilting, and overall free-motion designs such as stippling or other motif quilting that ignores the seamlines.

In-the-Ditch Quilting

In-the-ditch quilting works best for quilts in which you have pressed the seams to one side. It does not work well for seams that are pressed open. To quilt in the ditch, stitch along the

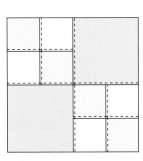

Quilting in-the-ditch

seamline between patches, making the stitches on the side of the seam without seam allowances. This avoids the bulk of the seam allowances so that you do not have to quilt through them. Since you simply follow the seamlines, there is no need to mark the quilting lines.

Outline Quilting

For outline quilting, stitches run parallel to the seamlines and are ¼" away and inside of the patch. This is effective for quilts with blocks that have lots of patches. I like to use outline quilting on Lone Star quilts because I press these seams open, making in-the-ditch quilting difficult to do. Quilting ¼" inside the seamline allows you to avoid stitching through more layers of fabric than necessary. For added emphasis, quilt another line of stitching ⅛" inside the first line.

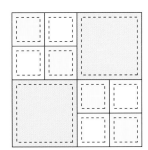 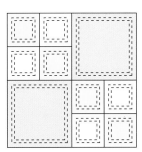

Outline quilting   Additional lines for emphasis

Echo Quilting

Echo quilting is executed by simply following the outline of a quilting motif, pieced patch, or appliqué pattern a specified distance from its outer edge. It is most effective when the designs being echoed have interesting outlines. I like to echo quilt in rows that are ¼" apart from each other.

 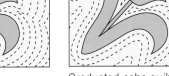

Echo quilting   Graduated echo quilting

You can create an interesting ripple effect by gradually increasing the distance between the lines of echo quilting as they move out from the motif.

Audition echo-quilted lines by drawing your central motif on paper. Then make several photocopies and doodle echoed lines on the photocopies. Choose the style you like best.

Overall Designs

Overall designs, like free-motion stippling and other patterns, require no marking. Machine quilters simply stitch the motifs or patterns without following any pre-marked lines. For hand quilting, you may prefer to mark the stitching lines freehand before stitching them.

Stipple quilting

Free-motion motif quilting

Marking as You Go

Some designs are best marked after the quilt sandwich is basted, thus avoiding the problem of markings that rub off or disappear over time. Single simple motif patterns, like hearts, can be easily marked using a prepared template or stencil. To mark as you go, position the template or stencil in the area to be quilted and trace the pattern. Overall quilting designs like clamshells or Baptist fan can be marked this way. When using this method, I prefer to mark only the portion of the quilt that fits in my hoop or frame, and quilt the motifs before repositioning the hoop and marking again. To facilitate the marking process, I like to pull the quilt taut in the hoop before marking, then loosen it slightly before beginning the quilting process. You can also place the quilt on a solid flat surface like a table to mark.

Straight-line quilting can be marked on the quilt top before basting or as you go. When straight lines are used as background stitching behind fancy motifs, I prefer to stitch all the fancies first, and then add the straight-line background fillers with a plastic see-through drafting ruler and marking pencil as I go. I don't usually mark every line, but will mark a line every inch or so, and "eyeball" the lines in between when I stitch them.

To mark straight lines, lay the quilt flat on a hard surface, preferably one that is at least large enough to accommodate the immediate area you are marking. Position the ruler on the quilt. For lines that run at a 45° angle on the quilt, align the 45° line on the ruler with a border seam or other straight seam. For lines that run parallel to seams, align one of the lines on the ruler with the seam. Run the marking pen or pencil along one edge of the ruler. Do not mark through the previously quilted motifs.

Elsie's Advice
Use a see-through drafting ruler, if you have one, for marking straight lines. They are thinner and more flexible than rotary cutting rulers, making them easier to use for quilt marking. If you use a rotary cutting ruler, be sure to hold your pencil perfectly perpendicular to the edge of the ruler.

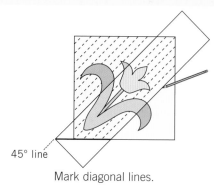
45° line
Mark diagonal lines.

If your ruler does not have a 45° line, simply make sure the seam runs diagonally from corner to corner within the square inches marked on the ruler.

For ¼" or ½" lines or cross-hatching, move the ruler and align the ¼" or ½" line with the previously drawn line. Continue moving, aligning, and marking in the same manner until the entire area is marked.

Stop and double check for 45° alignment every third or fourth line. This is important because it is easy to veer off slightly, and if not corrected continuously, your lines will quickly go askew.

Diagonal lines

Double diagonals

Crosshatching

Marking Before You Baste

Fancy designs are best marked before the quilt is basted and include feather patterns, recognizable objects or motifs, geometrics, cables, vines, and so on. These designs must be precisely stitched to get the full effect, and are most prominent when stitched in plain alternate blocks and borders made from solid fabrics or fabrics that read as solids. Busy prints camouflage beautiful, intricate quilting designs.

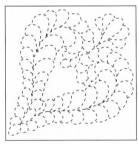
Feathers

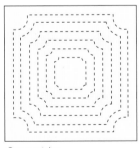
Geometrics

Cables

Freezer-paper Magic

There are hundreds of different stencil and template designs to choose from in quilt shops and mail-order catalogs. However, they never quite fit my quilts, so I usually end up having to struggle with them, adapting and shifting them to fill the areas of my quilt where I want them.

To fit commercial quilting patterns or stencils on my quilt, I find it easier to first redraft them on freezer paper cut to the size of the area of the quilt where I intend to use them. Then I mark my quilt.

Freezer paper was originally engineered for wrapping food for long-term cold storage. One side is paper (the dull side); the other side is coated with a plastic layer that acts as a vapor barrier to protect food from freezer burn. It is this back part of the freezer paper that sticks to fabric when pressed in place with a hot, dry iron. Quilters have found many uses for this product, from appliqué templates to quilting designs.

To adhere freezer paper to fabric, position it shiny side down on the fabric. Press on the paper side with a hot, dry iron, and the freezer paper adheres to the fabric until you purposely pull it off. Freezer paper doesn't leave any sticky residue on the fabric as may be the case with contact paper, tape, or other adhesives. This property makes freezer paper perfect for many quilting applications. Plus, it comes in 18" widths and in lengths up to 150 feet, so entire border designs can be drawn on it. It is readily available—you can buy it at most grocery and discount stores—and it is inexpensive, so you don't have to feel guilty about throwing out any mistakes you make along the way.

Freezer paper works well for tracing patterns from books, stencils, or even for drafting your own original designs. You can then use the freezer paper as the master pattern. I call this the marking guide. Adhere the marking guide to the wrong side of the quilt top, and it is then a simple task to trace and transfer the master design to the quilt. The freezer-paper pattern can then be re-used until the paper does not stick any longer.

Making and Using a Freezer-paper Marking Guide

1. Cut a piece of freezer paper the shape and size of the block or border(s) you intend to mark.

2. Trace the quilting designs in pencil onto the paper side of the freezer paper, making alterations as needed to fit the blocks or borders. Remember asymmetrical designs will appear reversed on the finished quilt top. When you like what you've drawn, darken the pencil lines with a black Sharpie fine-line marker. I prefer to use a Sharpie for this step for several reasons: The ink bleeds through the paper side of the freezer paper, stopping at the vapor barrier. Thus, the design is almost as visible on the underside as on the top side of the freezer paper. The ink is permanent and heat does not affect it, so it will not smudge or rub off on the quilt top. These qualities are important for the next few steps.

3. After the design is darkened on the marking guide, lay the quilt top wrong side up on an ironing board or other padded ironing surface, positioning it so that the portion of the quilt to be marked is laying flat. Place the marking guide, shiny side down in position on the quilt top, and adhere it to the quilt top by pressing it with a hot, dry iron.

Elsie's Advice
Do not use steam for this step because moisture causes the freezer paper to bubble and prevents it from sticking to the fabric.

4. Move the quilt top from the ironing surface to a lightbox or large window for tracing. You can turn a dining table into a large lightbox by removing the leaf and placing a piece of plate glass with masking-taped edges over the opening. (Some people use Plexiglas for safety reasons, but I found that the surface flexes too much, making it difficult to mark my quilts.) Tape the corners of the glass to the table and position a small lamp under the opening in the table. Turn on the lamp, and you have a large lit surface for marking your quilt top. To avoid scorching the quilt top, be sure to keep it away from the lit lamp bulb.

5. Place the quilt top right side up on the light source, and trace the design directly onto the quilt's surface, using a marking tool of your choice. Refer to Choosing Marking Tools at right for information on markers.

Note that some people prefer to use a patio door or other large window. Simply tape the quilt with the mark-

ing guide adhered to it over the window, and trace. If you are marking an area of the quilt made from light colored fabric, you might not need a lightbox to trace the design.

6. Once the entire design is marked, remove the marking guide. Reposition and adhere it to another section of the quilt for marking. The marking guide can be repositioned up to a dozen times. I've even used the same one for marking more than one quilt top. After I'm finished, I roll the marking guides up like wallpaper rolls and store them in open-topped boxes in my studio. These used marking guides are a great record of the quilts I have made, and they provided the basis for the quilting designs featured in this book.

Choosing Marking Tools

I am always asked what I use to mark my quilts, especially the ones with black backgrounds. Because there are so many new marking tools to choose from, quilters are always seeking the best one. Let me share my philosophy of marking tools.

First, I look for a marking tool that makes a line that is very fine yet is clearly visible in most lighting conditions. This is important since I quilt mostly in the evenings. To quilt an accurate line, it must be possible to follow the marked lines without straining to see them.

Second, the lines traced onto the quilt top before basting must stay visible until I choose to remove them. Sometimes, my quilts are in process for months or even years. It is important that the lines do not rub or wear off, or simply disappear with time.

Third, the markings must come out when the quilting is completed. Quilt judges certainly don't want to see any traces of quilt marks when a quilt is entered in national-level competitions, and neither do I!

These criteria eliminate several good marking tools from my repertoire. This doesn't mean they aren't perfectly satisfactory marking tools or that I never use them. It simply means that when I'm making a quilt for competition, I probably wouldn't choose to use them. Following is a discussion of several marking tools or methods and the circumstances under which I think they are best used. See the Resources list on page 111 for suppliers of my favorite markers.

• **Masking tape and self-stick templates.** Anything that feels sticky to touch may leave a residue on the fabric if left on for more than 24 hours. Tape works well for marking and quilting straight lines only if you are very careful to lay it straight when applying it to the quilts' surface. I find that if I stitch too close to tape, my needle picks up some of the adhesive, making if difficult to pull the needle through the fabric. When I use tape, I like to quilt at least 1/16" away from the edge. Remove all the tape when you are finished quilting for the day. Do not leave it on your quilt overnight.

• **Water-soluble markers.** These make perfectly visible lines that will stay visible for a very long time—at least in the semi-arid climate of southwest Kansas. In humid climates, they may lighten or disappear in times of high humidity. They are easily removed when the quilting is finished, as long as they are not heat set. Since the ink from these markers becomes permanent with heat, and I use an iron to adhere my marking guides, I cannot use these markers with my freezer-paper method. If the iron slides off the edge of the marking guide onto an already marked area, that area will become heat set. I have used water-soluble markers to mark backgrounds for appliqué, but I'm very careful never to expose the marking to heat. To fully remove the marks, the piece must be submerged in clean COLD water without adding any detergent or soap. Simply spritzing with water may cause the lines to disappear but they may ghost back as blue clouds on the quilt's front or back. Spritzing with water may merely drive the ink into the batting layer to reappear elsewhere later.

Elsie's Advice

If you mark your quilt with a water-soluble marker, don't leave your quilt anywhere where it will get quite warm. I discovered the hard way that leaving an unfinished, marked quilt in a car during a typical summer day can heat set these marks.

• **Chalk markers.** Chalk lines are quite visible on dark fabrics, but not on light colors. Since chalk lines tend to rub off or disappear over time, these markers are best used for mark-as-you-go techniques. Since you'll quilt the marked section in a short period of time, long-term visibility is not important. I do not recommend use of any of the colored chalk markers or powders that are visible on light fabrics. They sometimes leave pigment in the fabric that is difficult, if not impossible, to remove.

• **Colored marking pencils.** I choose not to use these for marking quilts because I've had trouble removing the pigment from some quilt tops. Yellow and pink seem to be the most difficult colors to remove.

• **Mechanical pencils.** I use mechanical pencils most of the time. The one I prefer is called the "Quilter's Ultimate Marking Pencil." It makes a fine line that is visible, and I never have to stop in the middle of marking a project to sharpen my pencil. The lines stay on the fabric until I remove them and I have been able to remove most marks after the quilting is done. However, the lines can be difficult to remove if marked too heavily.

Removing Marks

I suggest that you always use a very light hand when marking your quilt. Remember that what goes on must come off eventually. Products that do a good job of removing pencil lines from quilts include Sew-Clean and Marking Pencil Removal for Hobby, Crafts, Sewing, and Quilting.

To remove marks with these products, mist the marks on the quilt until quite damp, even to the point of being wet. Let the solution soak in for ten or fifteen minutes. If the marks are still visible, you may need to scrub them lightly with a soft toothbrush or your thumbnail. Then launder the quilt. Refer to Laundering on page 36 for details.

• **Nonce white marking pencil.** This is the tool I prefer for marking black quilts. This pencil has a soft, white lead that makes visible marks without dragging or damaging the fabric, but it does need frequent sharpening. Nonce pencils are inexpensive, so I buy them a dozen at a time, and sharpen them all at once. When I am marking a large quilt, I mark with one until it is dull, pick up another sharpened pencil and continue marking. When I've gone through all twelve pencils, I sharpen them all at the same time.

Elsie's Advice
Because sharpening pencils with small hand-held sharpeners is hard on the hands, and sharpening with a school-type wall-mounted sharpener is tedious, I purchased a battery-operated pencil sharpener. I think it was a worthwhile investment. It is quick and portable. I can take it along to sharpen pencils in the car if I choose.

The Nonce pencil's white lines stay visible for up to two years, the longest period of time I've spent quilting a quilt, but the marks will rub off easily with a dampened washcloth when the quilting is finished. If you make a mistake while marking, rub the marks off with a damp cloth. Wait until the quilt top is dry to re-mark that portion of the quilt.

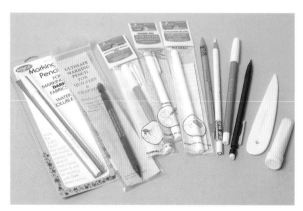

An assortment of marking tools

Adapting Quilting Designs for Machine Quilting

Most of the quilting patterns provided in this book can be easily adapted for machine quilting. The major difference between machine and hand quilting is that in machine quilting, starting and stopping a line of stitches is tedious at best. It is difficult to keep both sides of

the quilt looking tidy due to all the thread ends and lumps that can develop when a line of stitching begins or ends. Machine stitching threads cannot be run through the batting layer when moving from one area to the next, so it is important that the quilting be done in continuous, unbroken lines whenever possible. While you can leave long thread ends and use a needle to bury them in the batting by hand, you still want to minimize the number of thread ends you need to bury.

For example, feather quilting is executed differently for machine stitching. Parts of the feathers must be stitched over to get from point A to point B. For hand quilting, the thread is simply run through the batting layer to move from point A to point B.

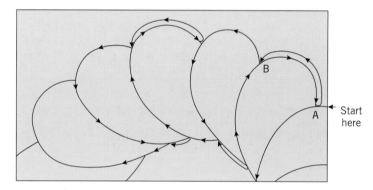

Machine quilting

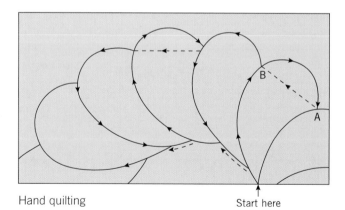

Hand quilting

Sometimes quilting lines can be eliminated or added, or motifs can be moved closely together to accommodate machine quilting. In this apple border design, for example, by moving the apple motifs close together so that they touch, each side of the design can be stitched continuously by machine without stopping and starting more than once.

Look for designs that can be traced without lifting your pencil from the paper. Sometimes designs, like this star border, can be stitched in two passes of your machine.

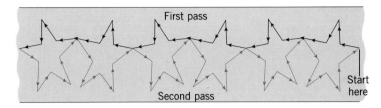

Take inspiration from hand quilting designs, but understand that the machine-quilted version does not have to be identical to get the same effect as hand quilting. Look for the possibilities and use your imagination. Another way to adapt feather quilting for easy machine quilting is to separate the feathers so that you won't have to overlap your stitching exactly.

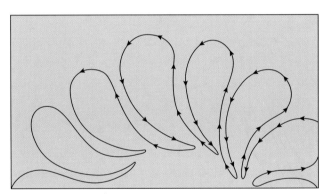

Feathers adapted for easy machine quilting.

There are lots of great books on machine quilting. Most of them will provide details about adapting quilting designs for machine work. If you are interested, see the list of books in the Bibliography on page 110.

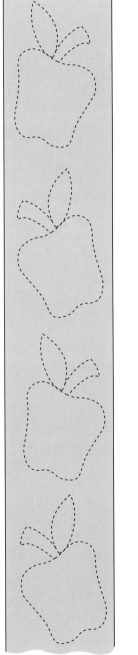

Single motifs for hand quilting

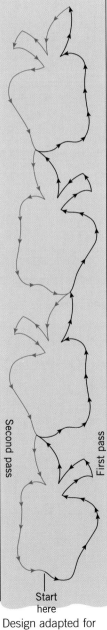

Design adapted for machine quilting

Stitching Up a Storm

I have heard it said that as long as you cannot catch your toe in the stitches, the quilting is serving its purpose of holding the three layers of the quilt together. Ideal quilting stitches are evenly spaced, with the stitches and the space in between those stitches being the same length. Near-perfect stitches will also be evenly spaced on the underside of the quilt.

In this chapter are tips and techniques that I hope you'll find useful for improving your hand quilting stitches. But before you take that first stitch, you need to make some informed decisions about fabric, batting, needles, and other products that will make hand quilting easier. Let's start at the beginning with fabric.

Machine quilting has some different requirements with regard to batting, basting, and, quilting. If you plan to machine quilt, I suggest that you consult one of the books listed in the Bibliography on page 110, or consult the staff at your favorite quilt shop.

Fabric

Fabric choices are critical for hand quilting. Choose a good quality cotton fabric that feels soft in addition to having a high number of threads per square inch. It should drape nicely when you handle it. If you can see the outline of your hand through the fabric, the thread count may be too low to hold up well in a quilt.

If you want your quilting stitches to be distinctive and highly visible, construct your quilt from solid color fabrics or fabrics that read as solids. I like to use prints in pieced areas of my quilts, and solid fabrics in large areas that I reserve for fancy quilting, such as setting triangles, alternate plain squares, and outer borders. Busy prints disguise stitches, but may provide outlines that you can quilt around without marking. In *Pharoah's Phans* on page 53, the solid, light-colored setting triangles feature fancy quilting designs. The striped border print provided lines that were easy to quilt without marking.

Batting

Batting is essentially the part of a quilt that makes it a quilt! It provides the fluff between the layers that gives dimension to the quilted designs and provides warmth. Put as much time and consideration into choosing your batting as you have the other materials used in your quilt.

The properties of the batting you choose are very important to the appearance and characteristics of your finished quilt. The batting can make hand quilting a joy or give you hours of struggle along the way. There is no one batting that is best for every quilt. Before choosing your batting, consider these questions.

• **Will this quilt be hand or machine quilted?** When hand quilting, the thickness of the batting (loft), fiber content, and density all affect the hand quilting stitch. Generally, higher lofts require the needle to pick up more batting fibers with each stitch, resulting in larger stitches. Most cotton battings are high in density and give more resistance to the needle than a similar weight polyester batting. If you are an experienced hand quilter, cotton battings can yield very satisfactory results, despite being slightly more difficult to needle. For the finest hand quilting stitches, I prefer a wool batting or low-loft polyester batting. Both allow the needle to glide through almost effortlessly.

For machine quilting, cotton or cotton/polyester blends are my preferred choice. The cotton fibers in the batting tend to hold onto the quilt top and backing. This keeps them from slipping and distorting during the quilting process and the quilt is less likely to develop puckers and pleats on either side.

• **Will this quilt be shipped across the country for shows?** If your quilt is made specifically to show in competitions, you'll want a batting that resists creasing and retains its shape with little or no stretching or sagging. Resilience is very important. Polyester is quite resilient, but it can beard, showing up as white fibers or balls of fuzz, especially on the surface of a dark quilt. Wool is easy to hand quilt, resists wrinkling and creasing, but is more expensive than polyester or cotton. It also beards when used with dark fabrics. A cotton/polyester blend has performed the best for me in dark quilts, but it is slightly more difficult to hand quilt than 100% polyester.

• **Will this quilt be laundered frequently?** In general, polyester battings launder well and dry more quickly than their natural-fiber counterparts. Some battings shrink when washed. Wool and silk battings may require dry cleaning. However, most wool battings have been preshrunk and are machine washable. See Laundering on page 36 for further information on washing quilts.

• **Do you prefer a flat, antique look for this quilt, or a puffier appearance with more definition of the quilting design?** In general, cotton batting gives the flatter, puckered look of antique quilts. Cotton needs to be quilted more closely than polyester to hold the batting fibers in place, or the batting tends to migrate, forming lumps of batting inside the quilt after washing. Cotton/polyester blend battings help to eliminate this problem. Both wool and polyester battings have more resilience and give more relief to the quilting designs.

Batting for Bed Quilts

If the quilt is specifically made for use as a bed quilt, you need to consider other issues as well.

• **Does the person who will use this quilt have any significant allergies to the fibers or chemicals used in the batting?** People who are allergic will need to launder their quilts more frequently and in hotter water, so the products used in the quilt must be top quality for

Batting samples top row, left to right are needle-punched cotton; high-loft polyester; charcoal polyester; regular-loft polyester; cotton/polyester blend; bottom row, left to right: wool; cotton with scrim; low-loft polyester; low-loft cotton; hollow-core polyester.

durability. Polyester is usually a good choice for allergic individuals, but is more apt to beard with frequent launderings. Organically grown and processed cotton battings are reported to be hypo-allergenic.

• **How comfortable will this batting be to sleep under?** Cotton wicks body moisture away, making it very comfortable in all weather conditions. Wool is very warm in cold climates. Polyester and other synthetic fibers can be quite comfortable when coupled with a cotton top and backing.

Bearding

Bearding can be a major problem in quilts. When long fibers from the interior layer of a quilt work through the surface of the quilt, one of two things happens. Either the fiber breaks off and disappears, or the fiber stays near the surface and makes a little ball or "pill." Sometimes, the quilt looks like it has sprouted little hairs all over it. Any batting you choose should be treated in some manner to prevent fiber migration or bearding. For more detailed information about battings, refer to the Bibliography on page 110.

Layering and Basting for Hand Quilting

Mark your quilt top, if you are marking before basting. Refer to Marking the Quilt on page 11 for further information on marking methods and markers.

Piecing the Backing

Prepare the backing fabric by prewashing and pressing it. The backing should be 4" or more larger than the quilt top. If the backing needs to be pieced, it is preferable to have two seams on either side of the center rather than a single seam that is dead center. This reduces stress on one seam, especially if the quilt is folded in half. To make a pieced backing for a quilt that is wider than 40" but less than 80" wide, you will need backing yardage that is two times the length of your quilt plus at least 8" extra.

1. Prewash and iron the fabric. Fold it in half across the length of the fabric, lining up the selvage edges.

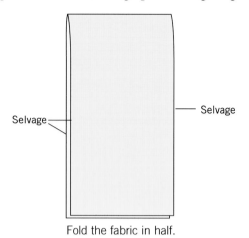

Selvage — — Selvage

Fold the fabric in half.

2. Stitch a ½" seam along each lengthwise edge. If the selvage marks are wider than ½", stitch a wider seam.

Stitch along the edges.

3. Trim the seams to ¼", trimming off the selvages.

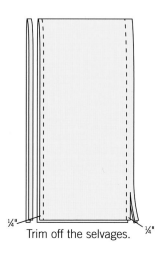

¼"   ¼"

Trim off the selvages.

4. Cut across the fold, and press the side seams open.

Cut across the fold.

5. Re-fold the tube of fabric so that the seams lay on top of each other, and cut along one side. Open up the backing. It is now ready to be sandwiched and basted.

Cut along one side.   Open up the backing.

Elsie's Advice

If you plan to do machine quilting, lightly starch the backing fabric during the final pressing. This will make the quilt slide easily over the machine bed.

For quilts that are wider than 80", stitch three lengths of fabric together and remove equal widths from the sides so that two of the seams are the same distance from the edges.

Basting the Layers Together

A large, rectangular table makes basting easier. I prefer one that is at least 60" in length and narrow enough so that I can reach to the center easily. Use masking tape, clothespins, or binding clamps to anchor the backing to the table. Protect your finger with a thimble. For less wear and tear on your hands, use long, thin needles such as milliner's, darning, or doll, and a large spoon to catch the needle point.

Useful tools for basting a quilt

1. Find the exact center of your worktable. Mark the center by taping toothpicks in the middle and the centers of the sides of the table, as shown. The toothpicks make it easy to find the exact center of the table through the quilt layers later.

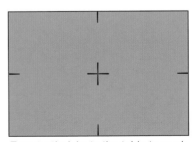

Tape toothpicks to the table to mark the centers.

2. Fold the pressed backing in half, right sides out. Then fold it in quarters.

Fold the backing in half, then in quarters.

3. Align the folded center of the backing with the center of the worktable and carefully unfold it. NOTE: When unfolded the backing will be wrong side up.

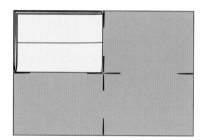

Center and unfold the backing on the table.

Elsie's Advice

For large, bed-sized quilts, enlist a friend to help with the layering and basting. Or throw a basting party, and serve dessert when the basting is done. Put on some music and enjoy what may otherwise be a tedious process.

4. Smooth out the backing, eliminating any bubbles or wrinkles. For small quilts that fit entirely on the top of the table, secure the backing to the table with masking tape. For larger quilts, secure the backing to the table with binder clips or clothespins.

Elsie's Advice

Since I struggle to open binder clips wide enough to fit on the edge of my table, I prefer to use clothespins. I simply gather up the extra backing that extends beyond the table's corner and clip it with a clothespin. My mother did this to secure picnic tablecloths on windy days.

Secure the backing to the table with a clothespin.

5. Fold the batting in quarters and center it on the table over the backing. Use the toothpicks to locate the center. Unfold. Do not secure the batting to the table. Smooth and pat out any bubbles or wrinkles. If the bubbles are too large to pat out, mist them with water and wait an hour or so for the batting to relax.

6. Fold the quilt top in quarters, wrong side out. Align the center with the middle of the table as you did the backing and batting. Use your fingertips to feel for the toothpicks to locate the center.

7. Unfold the quilt top, being careful not to disturb the batting and backing. The quilt top is right side up. Smooth the layers. At least 2" of the batting and backing should extend beyond the quilt top on all sides.

Elsie's Advice

Use only a light-colored thread for basting. I learned through experience that it is not wise to use dark colored thread for basting. One of my early quilts has tiny pink dots on it from the dye transferred from the red thread I used for basting.

Basting a Grid

1. Begin basting in the center of the quilt. Thread a long needle (darner, milliner's, or doll) with the end of thread off the spool, but do not cut the thread. Take one or two approximately ½" to 1" long stitches through all three layers. Pull the thread through and continue pulling until the length of thread on the needle extends past the edge of the quilt top 4" or 5".

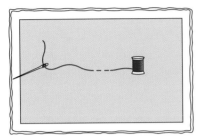

Begin basting in the center of the quilt. Do not cut the thread from the spool. Pull enough thread to extend past the edge of the quilt top.

Elsie's Advice
I make my basting stitches fairly small, about ½" long or less, so they don't catch on the wing nut of my quilting hoop or on buttons and other clothing items when I am quilting.

2. Continue basting in that direction to the edge of the table or end of the quilt top, whichever is shortest.

Elsie's Advice
Use a large spoon to catch the point of the needle, and needle grabbers, rubber fingertips, or office tacky dots to aid in pulling the needle through the layers. This will save your hands from fatigue.

3. When you reach the end of the table, but not the quilt, "park" the needle. Leave the needle pinned to the fabric to continue basting more of the quilt top later. If you've reached the end of the quilt, backstitch and cut the thread an inch or so from the quilt top. Be sure to cut the thread well above the quilt top so you don't accidentally snip a hole in your quilt (as I did one time).

4. Pull the thread from the spool end until the thread extends about 6" past the opposite edge of the quilt. Cut the thread.

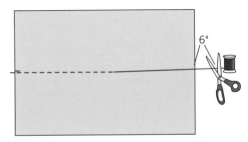

Cut the thread 6" beyond the quilt.

5. Thread a second needle with the cut end. Baste in the opposite direction. Park the needle or backstitch, as in Step 3.

6. Thread a third needle without cutting thread from the spool and stitch from the center of the quilt, perpendicular to the first line of stitching. Baste to the edge of the table or edge of the quilt. Park the needle or backstitch.

7. Pull the thread out from the spool end as in Step 4. Cut the thread, thread another needle, and baste in the opposite direction. You have now basted a large cross through the center of the quilt.

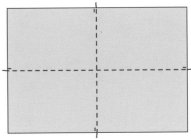

First lines of basting stitches

8. Baste parallel lines 3" to 4" on either side of the first lines. Continue basting until you have basted the quilt in a grid pattern over the entire area of the table. If it's a large quilt, you will have a needle parked at the edge of each line of basting. There are times when I have used as many as 50 needles at once for a large quilt.

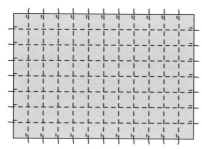

Basted grid on the tabletop

9. If the quilt is larger than the surface of the table, release the clothespins that secured the backing, and shift the quilt to one corner. Use the clothespins to secure the corners again. Pick up a parked needle and continue the basting line out to the outer edge. Secure the line of basting with a backstitch. Continue basting the remaining area on the table.

10. Shift the quilt to another corner, and baste. Continue shifting and basting until the entire quilt is basted in a grid.

Basting from the Center Out

Some quilters prefer to baste their quilts in radiating lines. Personally, I don't like the build-up of basting stitches in the center of the quilt. I like basting lines to

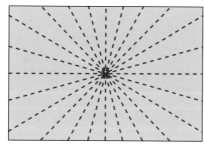

Build-up of basting stitches in the center

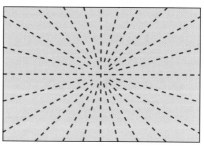

Begin additional lines farther out from the center.

be no further apart than 3". To make basting lines that close together along the outer edges, it takes a multitude of radiating lines to secure the layers of a large quilt. However, if you prefer this method, start several of the basting lines farther out from the center. Secure the ends with backstitches rather than knots. Knots tend to pull to the interior of the quilt, leaving large holes in the quilt's surface.

Basting the Edge

1. Run a row of shorter basting stitches approximately ¼" inside the outer edge of the quilt. These stitches should be ¼" or less in length.

2. Roll the excess backing and batting over the outer edge of the quilt top and baste in place. This prevents the batting edge from shredding and keeps the raw edge of the quilt top from unraveling during the quilting process.

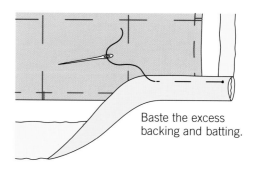

Baste the excess backing and batting.

Tools and Supplies for Hand Quilting

Before you begin hand quilting, you'll need a few specific tools. Selecting the right ones will make your work easier and more enjoyable.

Needles

The size and gauge (thickness) of a quilting needle directly affects the size of the quilting stitch. Quilting needles are different from those used for general sewing. *Sharps* are the kind usually used for appliqué or other stitching. *Betweens* are preferred for hand quilting; they are shorter by about ¼".

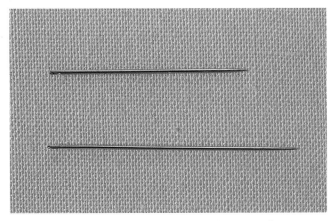

The Between or quilting needle on top is the same size or gauge as the Sharp or general sewing needle under it. Note the difference in length.

In general, the smaller the needle, the finer the stitch. I prefer to use a size 11 or 12 Between for hand quilting. Because the eye of a size 12 needle is very tiny, a needle threader is helpful. If you've never hand quilted before, begin with a size 9 or 10 needle. The thicker gauge makes these needles less likely to bend or break. Until you gain experience and learn to relax during the process, you may find that you bend the needles when executing the rocking stitch. This will improve as you learn how to bend the fabric around the point of the needle properly.

Elsie's Advice
I really like the size 11 needle sold under the brand name John James. Along with a larger, easier-to-thread eye, this needle has the gauge (thickness) of a size 10 needle coupled with the shorter length of the size 12.

Thimbles

Stitch length and evenness are controlled by the interaction between the fingers and thumb of your preferred hand above the quilt and the fingers of your non-preferred hand underneath the quilt. Because the eye-end of a fine needle is almost as sharp as the point, there is no substitute for a good, properly fitting *quilting* thimble. A typical quilting thimble has a raised rim that prevents the needle from sliding off.

A quilting thimble (on the left) has a rim around the top, while the sewing thimble (on the right) does not.

If you are a beginning hand quilter and are not comfortable with a thimble, try several different kinds. There are comfortable, flexible thimbles made from leather. Look for one with a reinforced tip. Other choices include self-stick thimble pads and tape, soft, thick plastic thimbles, and thimbles with openings for longer fingernails.

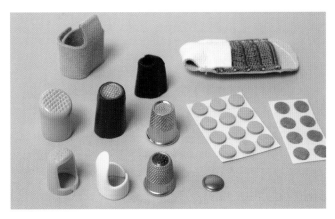

A variety of quilting thimbles

Quilting Thread

There are many different kinds of quilting thread on the market. I prefer a good quality 100% cotton thread. I avoid polyester and cotton-wrapped polyester threads. There is some discussion in the world of quilting that polyester, being a stronger and more durable fiber than cotton, may eventually cut through the cotton threads of the fabric as a quilt ages. I'd rather be safe than sorry.

Some quilting threads are glazed. Glazing is a process that thickens and smoothes the fibers of the thread, supposedly to make the thread glide more smoothly through the fabric. Glazed threads tend to be kind of wiry and thick. The thicker the thread, the harder it is to move through the fabric.

I prefer Mettler silk-finish 100% cotton mercerized sewing thread for quilting. It is the same thread I use to piece my quilts. It is strong enough to quilt with, doesn't tangle easily and comes in a multitude of colors. I do not wax my thread because wax residue can leave darkened holes in the fabric.

Use shorter lengths of thread, 18" or less, when quilting. You'll have to thread the needle more often, but using shorter lengths prevents the thread from wearing at the eye of the needle. Every time the needle passes through the quilt sandwich, stress is put on the thread at the eye, weakening it at that point.

Hoops

A quilting hoop is necessary to hold the basted quilt and free up both hands to work together to make perfect stitches. I heavily baste the quilt, then quilt it using a 14" wooden hoop. I learned to quilt at a large floor frame, but frames require that you sometimes stitch backwards—that is, away from yourself. This is very awkward and takes a lot of practice to make stitches that look as nice as those quilted toward you. With a hoop, the entire piece can be turned to stitch in any direction, so you are always quilting in the same direction.

As with most things in life, you get what you pay for when it comes to quilting hoops. Quality hoops are

made to last a lifetime, and are not cheap. The brackets for the nut and bolt of a quality hoop are attached to the outer hoop tightly. No staple ends are visible on the interior of a quality hoop. These can sometimes work loose and snag delicate fabrics. The wood on the cheaper hoop is soft and the hoop is unstable. Avoid purchasing a hoop like this. Note the smoothness and stability of the quality hoop. The slight striations are caused by the clamp used to secure the pieces while the glue was drying. If these are smooth, they are not a serious flaw in the hoop.

The good quality hoop is on the top and the cheaply made hoop is on the bottom.

Examine the wing nut. It should be large enough to make tightening it a comfortable task, and there should be no gaps where the bracket meets the hoop. There may be gaps and rough wood splinters at the bracket of an inexpensive hoop. Note the difference in the size and weight of the wing nut and bolt in the photographs.

The interior hoop is smooth without splinters, and the seam where the wood was joined is reinforced. If you spend a little bit more now, your quilting hoop will provide many years of service.

> ### Elsie's Advice
> *Quilting in a hoop also makes your work quite portable, enabling you to take it with you. I've been known to drag an in-progress quilt with me to little league games, doctor's offices, or wherever it is inevitable that I will have to wait.*

The seam of the interior ring of a quality hoop is reinforced with a brace (top) while the cheap hoop (bottom) is not.

Hand Quilting

You've finished the top, marked it for quilting, pieced the back, picked a batting, basted the three layers, and assembled your supplies. Now you're ready to quilt.

Place the Quilt Sandwich in a Hoop

Place the inside hoop on a table, and lay the basted quilt over it, positioning the hoop near the center of the quilt. Loosen the wing nut of the outer hoop until it slides easily over the quilt and the inside hoop. Tighten the wing nut slightly, then push your hand into the center of the hoop until it touches the table. This is the right amount of "play" or tension you'll need to make a good quilting stitch.

Push down to the table top with your hand to get the right tension.

The Quilting Knot

1. Thread the needle with an approximately 18" length of thread. Make a quilter's knot at the end of the thread you cut by grasping the thread tail between the needle point and index finger.

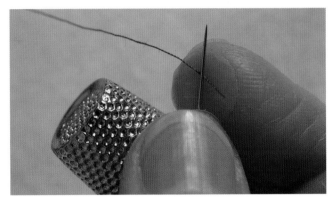

Grasp the end of the thread between the needle point and index finger.

2. While holding the thread tail, wrap the thread around the needle point 2 or 3 times. The number of times you wrap the thread will determine the thickness of your knot.

Wrap the thread around the needle 2 or 3 times.

3. Hold the thread wraps in place, and pull the needle through the wraps.

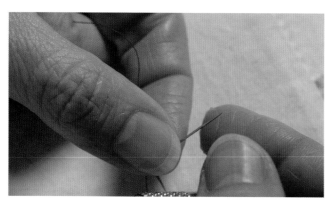

Hold the thread with the left fingers, and pull the needle through the wrapped thread.

4. Keep pulling until a small knot forms at the end of the thread.

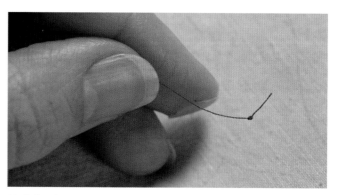

Pull the thread wraps until a small knot forms at the end of the thread.

5. Insert the needle into the fabric about ½" away from where you wish to start quilting. Pass the needle through the batting layer only, coming up exactly at the point where you wish to start stitching.

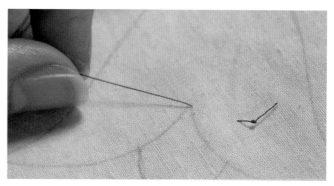

Bring the needle out where you want to start stitching.

6. Pop the knot through the quilt top into the batting layer by tugging gently, using a fingernail to assist, if needed.

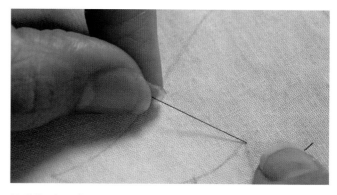

Pull the knot into the batting layer.

The Quilting Stitch

Now, you're ready to take the first stitch. The following instructions will show you how to execute a rocking-style quilting stitch. To make an even stitch, the needle must pierce the quilt sandwich at a 90° angle (perpendicular) with each stitch. Since the needle is not flexible, the fabric must be "bent" around the point of the needle. Rocking the needle from a straight up and down position to one that lies parallel with the quilt, and back to perpendicular allows your hands to work together to position the fabric so that the needle will pierce all three layers in a straight line.

1. Position the non-preferred hand under the starting point; insert the needle from the top perpendicular through the point where the thread exits the fabric. I try to stitch exactly on top of the thread as it exits the fabric or slightly behind that point. This anchors the thread and prevents what looks like a stitch that pops up slightly where the stitches from one length of thread stop and start.

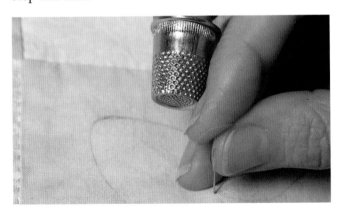

Insert the needle straight down just behind where the thread exits the fabric.

2. As soon as you feel the point of the needle exiting on the underside of the quilt, STOP pushing. Transfer the eye end to the thimbled finger and let go of the needle. Control the needle's movement through the quilt by pushing up slightly with your fingers on the non-preferred hand from the underside of the quilt and down with the thimble. Understand that however far the needle exits the quilt on the underside will determine how long the underneath stitch will be.

Use the thimble to control the needle's movement through the quilt.

3. With the thimbled finger, rock the needle into a horizontal position. Place the thumb of the upper hand in front of the point just ahead of where you expect the needle point to appear. Push down slightly on the fabric with your thumb while pushing the point of the needle up from the underside with the finger underneath, creating a little "hill" of quilt sandwich in front of the needle point.

Create a little "hill" in front of the needle point.

4. When the fabric is perpendicular to the needle, push the needle through the hill until you just see or feel the point of the needle exiting the quilt top. Stop pushing.

Watch for the point of the needle to emerge from the quilt top.

5. With the thimbled finger, rock the needle back into the vertical position and repeat this process.

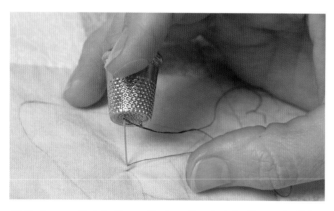

Rock the needle into the vertical position to take the next stitch.

6. Load several stitches on the needle in this manner. If you are a beginner, take only 1 or 2 stitches at a time. As you gain experience, you may be able to load as many as 5 or 6 stitches on the needle at one time.

Take 1 or 2 stitches at a time if you are a beginner.

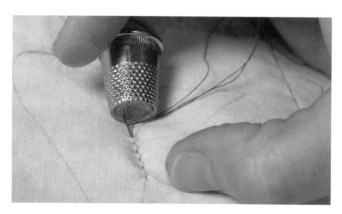

Load more stitches on the needle as you gain experience.

7. Pull the needle through. Estimate the next stitch placement and insert the needle perpendicular to the quilt and repeat the rocking stitch steps. Some quilters find estimating the next stitch to be the hardest part, but it gets easier with practice.

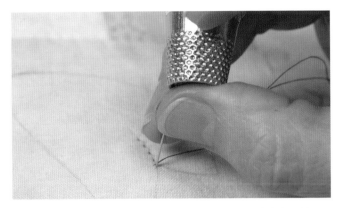

Insert the needle perpendicular to the quilt one stitch length away to start the next stitch.

Ending the Stitch

1. When you reach the end of a line of stitching, tie off by holding the needle point close to the surface of the quilt near the last stitch taken. Wrap the thread 2 or 3 times around the needle close to the surface of the quilt, similar to the way you made the quilter's knot when you first threaded the needle.

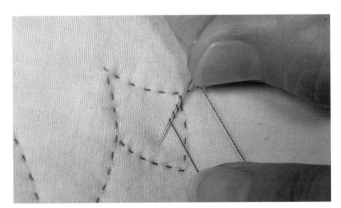

Wrap the thread 2 or 3 times around the needle.

2. Hold the wraps on the needle and pull the needle through the wraps until a small knot forms near the surface of the quilt.

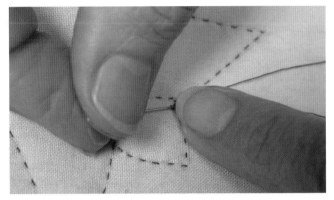

Hold the thread wraps and pull the needle to form a knot.

3. Pass the needle through the batting layer, coming up about ½" away.

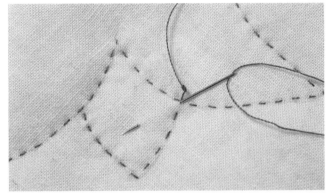

Bring the needle up about ½" away.

4. Pop the knot into the batting layer and clip the thread near the surface of the quilt. Work the thread end into the quilt.

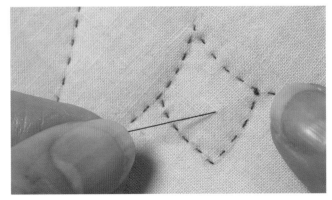

Pull on the knot to pop it into the batting layer.

Traveling

1. If you are close to the next starting point (1" or less), you may wish to "travel" to the beginning of the next quilting line. Estimate the last stitch placement and pass the needle through the batting layer, coming up about ½" away. Do not pull the needle completely out of the batting layer.

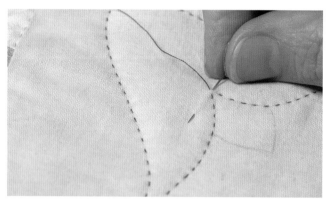

Bring the needle up about ½" away from the last stitch.

2. Turn the eye end of the needle in the batting layer toward the next starting point. Bring the eye end up through the quilt top without pulling the needle point end completely out of the batting layer.

Turn the eye end of the needle in the direction you are headed.

3. Turn the point end of the needle in the batting layer and repeat this process until you reach the next starting point. Pull the needle completely through the quilt top and begin stitching the next quilting line.

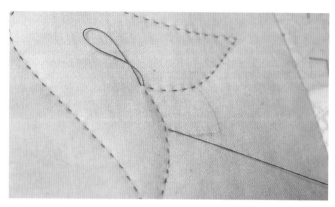

Bring the point of the needle out where you want to begin stitching; pull the needle and thread through.

A No-knot Method

Knots sometimes pop out to the surface of the quilt. There are some threads, such as metallics, that will not hold a knot. Since there are no knots to pop to the surface, this technique works well with slippery threads like silk or metallics.

1. Cut a double length of thread (about 35" to 40") and thread the needle. Begin stitching exactly on a design line, leaving about half the thread hanging loose.

Leave half the thread hanging loose.

2. Stitch along the quilting line in one direction. When only 4" or 5" of thread are left, or when ending a section of a design, pass the needle through the batting layer, bringing the point to the top, but without bringing the needle completely out of the quilt. The end of the needle should clear the line of stitches.

3. Run the eye end of the needle back in the batting layer through the line of stitching, bringing the eye end of the needle to the surface of the quilt. The point end of the needle should clear the stitching line but not exit the quilt.

4. Without pulling the needle completely out of the quilt, pass the point of the needle through the batting layer and through the next stitch.

5. Continue weaving the thread back and forth in the batting layer until the thread has been woven through 4 or 5 stitches. Then bring the needle up ½" away and completely through the fabric this time. Clip the thread close to the surface of the quilt.

Weave the thread back and forth in the batting and through the stitches.

6. Re-thread the needle with the long tail of thread left at the starting point and stitch in the opposite direction.

Thread the needle with the loose thread, and stitch in the opposite direction.

7. To tie off, weave the thread through the stitches, as before. Both ends of the thread are now secured without knots.

Solving Problems

When I teach hand quilting, there are several questions that I routinely get from quilters. Here are some frequently asked questions and the solutions I have found for these dilemmas.

• **What can I do if a knot pops to the surface of my quilt?** If this happens during the first few stitches, I would simply clip off the knot, pull the thread through and start over. If this happens on a finished quilt, or on a line of stitching that has progressed more than an inch or two, I pop the knot back into the batting layer in the following manner:

1. Cut a short length of thread, less than 6" long. Thread both cut ends through the eye of a needle. Insert the needle into the quilt top close to the knot, and exactly where the knot should go back into the fabric.

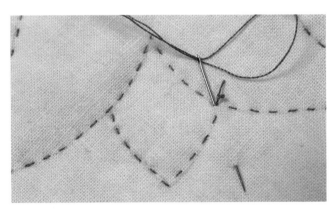

Insert the needle where the knot should go back into the fabric.

2. Traveling in the batting layer only, bring the needle up about ½" away. As the thread is pulled into the quilt, place the loop of thread around the knot, catching the knot at the surface of the quilt.

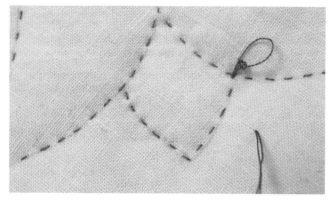

Place the loop of thread around the knot.

3. Gently tug on the thread and needle, popping the knot back into the quilt's interior.

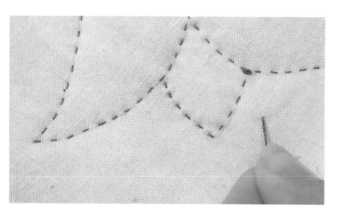

Pull on the thread to pop the knot back into the batting.

• **How can I hand quilt through bulky seam allowances?** There are two solutions to this problem. The first is simply to stab stitch through the seams, taking only a half a stitch at a time. You may need to turn the quilt over to estimate the stitches on the underside. Continue stitching in this manner until your line of stitches has cleared the seams.

Insert the needle straight down through the seam.

Turn the quilt over to insert the needle back to the top.

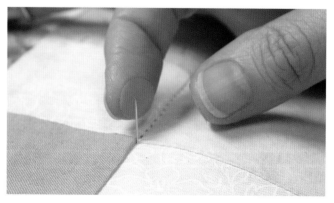

Pull the needle up from the top to complete the stitch.

A second way to negotiate seams is to take a single, longer stitch, making certain that the stitch goes through to the backing layer. Begin the next stitch behind the first stitch (backstitching.) Continue taking backstitches until you have passed the bulk of the seams.

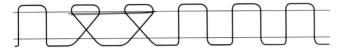

Backstitch through bulky seams.

• **When beginning a new length of thread in the middle of a line of stitching, I get an uneven-looking stitch that is quite obvious. What am I doing wrong, and how can these stitches be prevented?** I call these pop-up stitches because they do not pull the three layers of the quilt together. With the knotted end buried in the batting, they lie on the surface of the quilt, rather than creating an indentation like the previous stitches and subsequent stitches. The solution to this problem is to always end with a stitch forward into the batting layer only. Begin the next stitch with a newly threaded needle by going down through the batting layer exactly where the last thread enters the fabric.

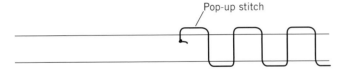

The stitch pops up because it is not anchored to the backing, thus there is not enough tension on it to make an indentation in the quilt top to match the preceding stitches.

Insert the needle perpendicular to the fabric exactly in the same place the thread exited the fabric, piercing the thread if possible.

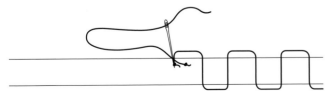

Pierce the thread if possible to anchor the stitch.

Then, stitch forward in the usual manner. This anchors the first stitch to the backing through the batting, and the resulting stitch does not pop up or lift up. The line of stitching will appear as one unified, continuous line of quilting.

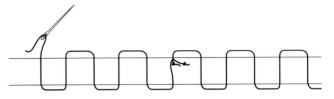

All stitches appear the same.

• **I have sore fingers. What can I do to help them heal so that I can continue to quilt comfortably?** Prevention is the best cure. Use some form of finger protection for your fingers. I like to use office tacky dots—the little plastic adhesive kind used for sorting papers. I put one on the underneath finger used to make the hill and feel the needle point as it exits the fabric. I can still feel the point, but the dot offers some protection. I also use the tacky dots on my right hand index finger and thumb to give me traction for handling and pulling the needle through the quilt layers. A small piece of adhesive tape, or a dry coating of clear fingernail polish also works well to protect the underneath finger.

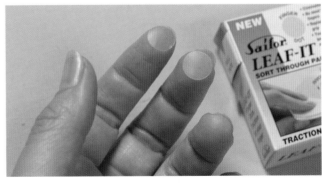

Use office tacky dots to protect your fingers.

After the fact, the only cure for sore fingers is rest. Some products that will aid healing include Udder Cream, Bag Balm, Gloves-in-a-Bottle, and pure lanolin. Bag Balm and lanolin are oily substances that will stain your quilt, so do not quilt after applying them.

Crossing the Finish Line

Congratulations! You've pieced and appliquéd, marked and basted, and finally finished hand quilting your heirloom quilt. What's next? It's tempting to hurry through the next few items on the agenda, but please take the time to do them right. They are as important as any of the preceding steps, and they may take almost as much effort.

Remove the Basting and Marking

First, remove the basting stitches. Take care when pulling out the basting; you don't want to disturb quilting stitches that may have caught the basting threads. If you feel resistance, stop. Check to see where the basting thread is caught. Carefully snip just the basting thread close to the quilting stitch, and remove the basting thread. Remove only the basting in the interior of the quilt. DO NOT remove the basting stitches holding the rolled edges of the backing over the quilt top edges.

It is imperative, especially if you plan to enter national competitions, that marking be completely removed. Depending on how heavily you marked, this step can go quickly or take some time. In many instances, if the quilting stitches lie exactly on a fine pencil line, the markings will disappear into the shadow left by the quilting stitches. If the marks are not evident, there is no need to remove them.

To examine the quilt for marks that need to come out, lay the quilt on a horizontal surface in good light—a large bed or table in a well-lit room or a room with lots of natural light. Examine every inch of the quilt closely. If you see any markings, they'll need to come out. The method to remove marks depends on the marking tool used.

Water-soluble Marker

If you used a water-soluble marking tool, fill a washing machine with cold water. The water must be cold, not warm or hot. Do not add detergent or soap because some laundry products can actually set the ink. Fully immerse the entire quilt in the water. Do not turn the machine agitator on, but simply move the quilt up and down in the water with your hands. Then set the machine to spin out the water; refill the tub with cold water a second time. Repeat the process of agitating by hand and spinning the water out. Two or three rinses should be sufficient. Proceed to Laundering if your quilt needs further cleaning or Blocking on page 37 if your quilt is ready to dry.

Nonce Marking Pencil

To remove the white Nonce marking pencil lines made on dark fabrics, dampen a light-colored washcloth with water. Gently rub the lines with the dampened washcloth, and they should wipe right off.

Mechanical Pencil

If you marked the quilt with the Quilter's Ultimate Marking Pencil or other mechanical pencil, spritz any obvious marks with a product such as Sew-Clean or Marking Pencil Removal for Hobby, Crafts, Sewing, and Quilting (available at quilt shops). Rub the mark gently with your fingertip or a soft toothbrush until it disappears. You may have to apply the remover solution a second time or even saturate the mark with it. When you are satisfied that the marks are gone, follow up with laundering.

Laundering

Sometimes it takes a year or more for me to finish the hand quilting on a large quilt. Needless to say, the quilt can be a bit dirty by the time I finish, especially if it traveled with me during the process. Since I always use new, good quality 100% cotton fabrics for my quilts, they will stand up to laundering. However, if your quilt is made from vintage blocks or fabrics, you may prefer to skip this step. Agitation is the part of the laundering process that wears textiles out. The abrasion of fabric rubbing against fabric can be harmful to your quilt, so proceed cautiously.

Fill a washing machine with tepid water. The water should not be hot or ice cold. Then add a mild quilt soap or detergent like Orvus Paste to the water and swish the water around a little to fully disperse the soap. NEVER use bleach or whiteners on quilts.

Turn the machine off and immerse the quilt in the water. Push the quilt up and down in the water by hand. If you wish, allow the quilt to soak for 10 or 15 minutes. Set the machine to the spin cycle, and spin out the wash water. Allow the machine to fill the tub for the rinse cycle, then turn the machine off, and push the quilt up and down by hand. Spin, and rinse a second time. If suds appear on the surface of the rinse water, rinse a third time and even a fourth time until you are certain the soap has all been rinsed from the quilt. Following the final spin cycle, remove the quilt from the washer, being careful not to stretch or pull on it. Support the wet quilt as much as possible because the weight of the water will make it very heavy. Any stress on the fine hand quilting stitches can break them or pop knots to the quilt's surface. Enlist a helper, if needed. Now you are ready to block the quilt.

Blocking

Blocking can correct for slight imperfections in the shape and size of the quilt. It's a little like blocking a piece of needlework, only the needlework here is very large indeed. A large open room with a carpeted floor works well, but you can use any flat surface that is large enough to support the entire length and width of the quilt.

First, protect the carpet from dampness by laying down a moisture barrier such as a couple of inexpensive plastic shower curtains. Then place a padded layer of old terrycloth towels, a king-sized mattress pad, or several clean sheets on the moisture barrier. This layer will absorb moisture from the damp quilt while it is drying.

Carefully lay the damp quilt over the layers, and gently work it into place, patting out wrinkles and bubbles, manipulating it to be perfectly square. Measure the center and sides of the quilt to make sure opposite sides are exactly the same size. Then measure the diagonals.

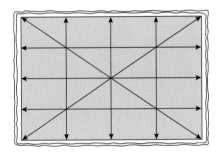

Elsie's Advice
Take blocking measurements with a metal, retractable measuring tape, not a dressmaker's tape measure. The metal tape stays stiff, making it much easier to measure across the expanse of damp quilt.

When opposite sides and the diagonal measurements are identical, you can be assured that the corners are a true 90°. Walk around the quilt and double check that all interior seam lines are straight. Examine these lines from a low angle, looking from side to side. Check diagonal lines, too. I sometimes straighten lines while the quilt is damp, holding the lines in place with pins stuck straight through the seams, padding, moisture barrier, and into the carpet below. I leave the pins in place until the quilt is nearly dry.

If you are not confident eyeballing the lines, purchase a piece of lattice or quarter-round at a home improvement store. It comes in 8' lengths and is great for checking straight lines. Gently place the lattice or quarter-round on the surface of the quilt along the lines. It will be obvious if the lines are not straight. Before using any wood products for checking straight lines, examine the piece for rough places or splinters. Sand it perfectly smooth and wipe off the sawdust before laying it on your quilt.

Release the basting that is holding the backing and batting around the outer edge of the quilt. Carefully unroll the backing and batting without disturbing the quilt and double-check the outer edges for straightness. Block the outer edges, using the lattice or quarter-round and pinning as needed to establish a straight line.

Cover the quilt with a clean sheet to protect it from possible wandering feet of any kind. If it is a warm day, open the windows and turn on a couple of fans to speed the drying process. It may take just a few hours for the quilt to dry, or up to twenty-four hours, depending on the humidity, temperature, type of batting used, and how efficient your washing machine is at spinning out water.

When the quilt is completely dry, remove any pins. I prefer to trim the outer edge even at this point. However, many quilters prefer to stitch the binding to the front of the quilt before trimming the excess batting and backing. Either way is fine.

To trim the excess backing and batting, lay the lattice piece along the outer edge and mark a straight line. Then cut along the marked line with scissors. Or, slide a rotary cutting mat under the quilt's edge and trim it with a rotary cutter and ruler while the quilt is still flat on the floor. Now the quilt is ready for binding.

Binding

Beauty is in the details, and binding is one of those details that may take a little practice and expertise to execute beautifully. I will share with you my techniques for making a simple, straight-grain double-fold French binding. For other edge finishes, refer to the Resource list for books on the subject.

Straight-grain Double-fold Binding

To figure how wide to cut strips for binding, decide how much binding you want to show on the front of your quilt. Triple that measurement and add ⅛" to ¼" for the loft of the batting. Double the total, and that is the width to cut the fabric strips for binding. For example, if you want a ¼" finished binding with a regular loft batting, you would cut 2"-wide strips (3 x ¼" = ¾"; ¾" + ¼"= 1"; 1" x 2 = 2"). Cut enough strips to go around your quilt and add at least 12" extra to account for corners and seams.

Making the Binding

1. Sew the binding strips together with diagonal seams. Place two strips right sides together at a right angle, and stitch on the diagonal as shown. Trim the seam to ¼". Press it open. Stitch all the binding strips into a single, long strip.

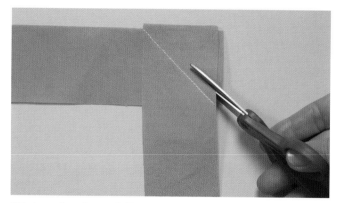
Stitch on the diagonal. Trim the seam to ¼".

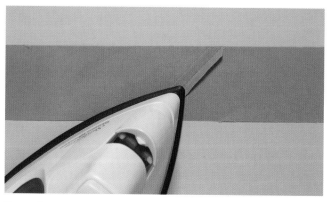
Press the seam open.

2. At the ironing board, press the binding strip in half lengthwise with right sides together. For a crisp, folded edge, give the strip a final pressing with steam or a light mist of water.

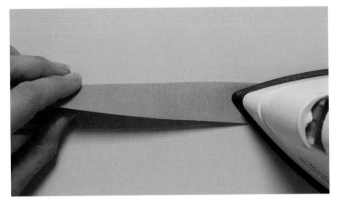

Press in half with right sides together.

3. Open one end of the binding. With a rotary cutter and ruler, trim one end at a 45° angle.

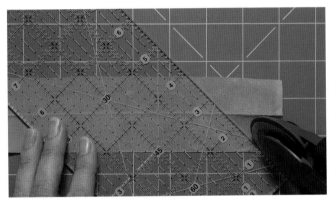

Trim one end at a 45° angle.

Attaching the Binding

When applying the binding, the outer edge of the quilt may stretch. To prevent this, measure the quilt through the center, the same as for adding borders. Then measure and pin the binding in place, matching centers and quarter marks. This takes a little more time, but without this step I've run into difficulty with outer edges that stretch and wave.

1. Measure the length of the quilt through the center. Divide the measurement in half. Measure that length of binding beginning about 4" from the trimmed end. Mark the starting and the ending points with pins; mark the quarter point, too, if desired.

Mark half the length with pins.

2. Pin the measured length of binding in place on the front of the quilt, beginning at the center of one long side of the quilt, matching the outer edge of the quilt and the raw edges of the binding. Leave the trimmed end free.

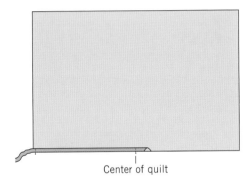

Pin the binding to the quilt.

3. Install a walking foot on your sewing machine, or use the even feed mechanism if your machine has one. Begin stitching at the center of the side. Stitch ¼" from the raw edges.

Use a walking foot to stitch the binding to your quilt.

4. Stop stitching exactly ¼" from the corner with the needle down. Turn the quilt 45° and stitch to the corner of the quilt. Clip the threads and remove the quilt from the sewing machine.

Stitch to the corner at a 45° angle.

5. Rotate the quilt, then fold the binding away from the quilt, forming a 45° fold in the binding. Fold the binding down, aligning the raw edges with the trimmed edge of the quilt, and aligning the second fold with the upper edge of the quilt.

Make a 45° fold in the binding.

Align the raw edge of the binding with the edge of the quilt.

6. Measure the width of the quilt through the center. Measure the binding to fit, and pin it to the quilt, matching the center of the binding with the center of the quilt. Pin the binding in place. Measure and match the quarter point of the binding, too, if desired.

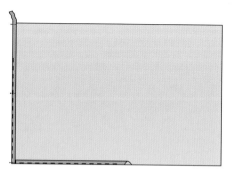

Pin the binding in place, matching centers.

7. Stitch, catching the mitered pleat in the corner. When opened out, the corner should form a miter only to the corner of the trimmed quilt top, as shown.

Stitched miter at corner

Miter opened out

8. Continue measuring, pinning, stitching, and turning the corners until you reach the side of the quilt where you started. Measure and pin the binding to the midpoint of the quilt. Stitch to within 8" of the starting point, stop, and backstitch. Clip the threads and remove the quilt from the machine.

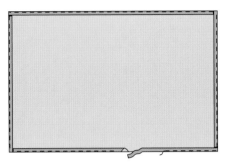

Stop stitching about 8" from the starting point.

9. Lay the binding flat against the quilt, overlapping the trimmed end. Open the bindings and fold the untrimmed end of the binding at a 45° angle to match the trimmed end. Finger press a crease. Trim the end of the binding ½" beyond the finger-pressed crease.

Finger press a crease at a 45° angle.

Trim ½" beyond the crease.

10. Stitch the trimmed ends of the binding with right sides together. Note that a V forms where the binding strips come together. Begin stitching in the V to form the seam. Finger press the seam open.

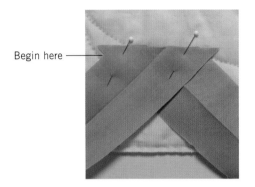

Begin here —

Begin stitching at the V.

Finger press the seam open.

11. Refold the binding and machine-stitch it to the quilt, overlapping both of the previous lines of stitching. Remove the quilt from the machine.

Finish stitching the binding to the quilt.

12. Fold the binding over the trimmed edge of the quilt, covering the machine stitching, and blindstitch the fold to the back of the quilt by hand. Form miters at the corners and stitch the miters shut for flat, neat corners.

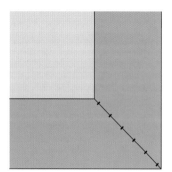

Stitch the miters.

Labeling and Documenting your Quilt

Please take the time to make a label for your quilt. Knowing the provenance of antique quilts can sometimes double their value. Your heirs will appreciate that you took the time to document your quilt.

When making your label, be sure to include your name, the date, and where you lived when you made the quilt. Other information that is important to include would be for whom you made the quilt, if it is a gift, and the occasion for which it was made. Where you got the inspiration for this quilt, or a little information about yourself as the quiltmaker would add to the quilt's story. Create the label with permanent ink or embroidery—something that will remain intact over the years. Then stitch it to the backing side of the quilt.

Because of theft of valuable quilts in recent years, I've begun to write this information in permanent ink directly on the back of my quilt. I stitch the fancy fabric label over the one written directly on the quilt. That way, if the label somehow falls off or is removed, the basic documentation is still there and is an integral part of the quilt. A thief would have to damage the quilt to remove it.

When I start a new quilt, I label a manila envelope with the tentative name of the quilt and the date.

Add a label to document your quilt.

Samples of the fabrics, appliqué templates, preliminary drawings and sketches, and other things that pertain to this particular quilt go inside the envelope. The date when the quilt was completed and other milestones are recorded on the outside. When the quilt is entered into shows, the show and date are written on the outside and if the quilt comes home with a ribbon or award, these are recorded, too. Judge's critiques, publication pages, and any other things pertaining to that quilt go into the envelope. I've also written the name of one of my sons on each envelope to indicate which one will eventually receive the quilt.

Gallery of Quilts

Welcome to the gallery of quilts. Here's a chance to be inspired by some stunning quilts and quilting designs. Study the quilting details in these quilts and give your imagination free reign to adapt the designs or create some that are your own unique originals. All the quilts featured in this gallery were constructed and quilted by Elsie M. Campbell unless otherwise noted in the description.

Cubic Stars
43" x 43", 2001

Graphic and colorful, this quilt brightened some long dark winter days while I was constructing it. Feather patterns grace the black areas surrounding the Broken Star center. Diagonal straight-line quilting in the borders provides a contrasting graphic pattern that gives more importance to the feathered motifs. This quilt received an Honorable Mention at the International Quilt Association's 2001 Show in Houston, Texas.

Great-Grandma Goebel's
Red & Green Appliqué Quilt
80" x 80", 1993

My great-grandmother Anna Risser-Goebel made a stunning red and green appliqué quilt in 1857 when she was only 18 years old. My mother first became aware of this quilt while attending a family reunion in 1989. The original quilt featured feathered wreaths between the large appliqué blocks and straight feather motifs in the borders. The appliqué blocks were crosshatched throughout. I decided to change the quilting patterns to fit my contemporary sense of design, adding hearts to the feathered wreaths and echo quilting around the appliqué motifs. Quilting designs can be found on pages 69 and 84.

1897 Fresco Stencil
76" x 93", 1997, by Hazel Canny

Hazel Canny's quilt is one of the most beautiful hand quilted whole-cloth quilts I've ever had the privilege of viewing. Hazel is a master of the wholecloth quilt, and consistently wins top awards each year in the Best Hand Quilting category at the International Quilt Association Show in Houston, Texas. This quilt was no exception, winning the IQA Founder's Award in 1997. The quilting patterns were inspired by a 19th-century stencil that Hazel's sister gave her. Please note the exceptional background quilting. Large grids are filled with straight-line diagonal quilting that creates chevrons where the grids meet. What a unique way to fill negative space with texture!

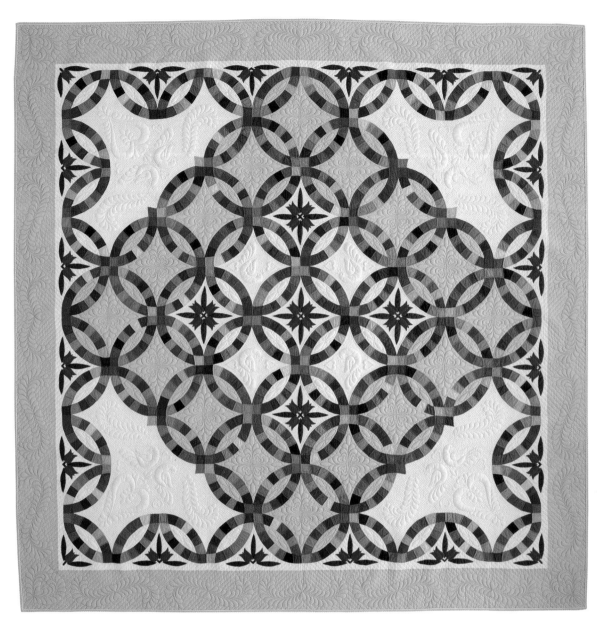

Tulip Garden Wedding
92" x 92", 1997

I love challenges and wanted to make a Double Wedding Ring quilt with a twist. I like to add simple appliqué to pieced quilts so I drafted the red tulips for the center of the blocks and borders. Trapunto was added to the feathered motifs with needle and yarn after hand quilting them. This quilt is from the collection of Jim and Sally Thomas. Quilting designs can be found on pages 86–87.

The Long Road to Baltimore
94" x 94", 1999, by Joan Streck

Joan Streck started this beautiful Baltimore Album quilt in 1991 while taking a hand appliqué class from teacher Beverly Gobel. It took nearly eight years from start to finish, thus Joan named this quilt appropriately. The work that author and teacher Elly Sienkiewicz has done with research and publication of historic Baltimore Album quilts inspired Joan along the way. Joan chose to incorporate my Peaches and Cream quilting patterns, pages 72–73, and 77, in the background of her quilt. This quilt won Best of Show at the 2001 Kansas State Fair and the 2003 National Quilt Association's show in Columbus, Ohio.

Aunt MiMi's Triumph
81" x 81", 2000

This quilt, also known as Whig's Defeat, took more than three years to piece because I became bored with the tedious precision machine piecing process. However, the quilting took a total of only five months to complete because I enjoyed it so much. Feather quilting and related motifs grace the scalloped borders. Among this quilt's list of awards are Best of Show at Quilt America! in Indianapolis in 2000, and the Mary Krickbaum Award for Best Hand Quilting at the 2001 National Quilt Association Show in Tulsa, Oklahoma.

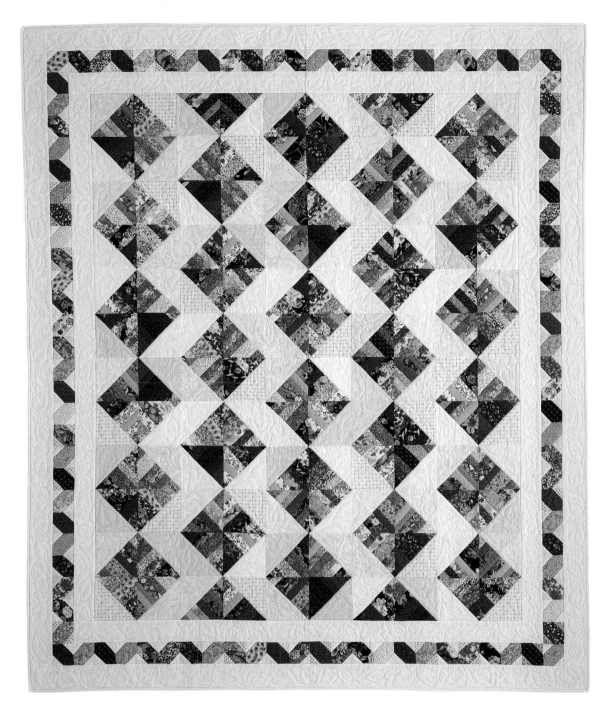

String Along With Me
79" x 90", 2002, by Phyllis Bean Enos

Inspired by a traditional string quilt pattern, Phyllis stitched her version from pastel prints and an assortment of white-on-white prints. For the quilting pattern, Phyllis simply drew free-hand leaves in the white triangles with her fabric marker. Machine quilters would free-motion quilt similar patterns, but Phyllis chose to quilt her designs by hand. This quilt won First Place, Traditional Large Pieced category at the 2003 Oklahoma City Winter Quilt Show.

Let Freedom Ring
54" x 54", 2002

Sometimes I have a great idea for a quilting design, and decide to create a quilt around the quilting pattern. Originally, the quilting pattern was used on a guild's fundraiser quilt, which was subsequently given away. When beginning this book, I wanted a quilt to showcase the eagle and Liberty Bell patterns used in that first quilt. *Let Freedom Ring* is the result. New York Beauty blocks set with sashing work together to create this stunning design. The patriotic color scheme is the ideal backdrop for the National Emblem Eagle and Liberty Bell quilting designs. Quilting designs can be found on pages 89–90.

Star Flower
83½" x 83½", 2002

Luscious hand-dyed fabrics make this a handsome masterpiece quilt that combines both piecing and appliqué. See Resources on page 111 for a pattern for the piecing and appliqué. Fabulous hand-quilted feather motifs add the finishing touch. The quilting designs can be found on pages 80–81. This quilt has earned several awards at major quilt shows across the country including: First Place and Viewer's Choice, Oklahoma City Winter Quilt Show, 2003; First Place Mixed Techniques category, Sew Near to My Heart Show, Cincinnati, Ohio, 2003; First Place Other Techniques category, Quilters' Heritage Celebration, Lancaster, Pennsylvania, 2003; the Best Hand Workmanship award at the AQS show in Paducah, Kentucky, 2003, and now resides in the permanent collection at the Museum of the American Quilter's Society.

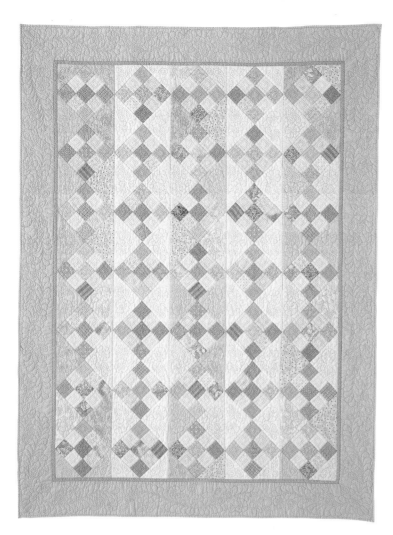

Peaches and Cream
42" x 64", 2003

The quilting pattern for *Peaches and Cream* is subtle but enriches this simple scrap quilt. Blossoms, paisleys, and hearts are superimposed over a feathered cable design in this beautiful pattern. You'll find several different variations of this pattern beginning on page 72.

Fandango
24" x 57½", 1992, by Helen Storbeck
Quilting designs and hand quilting by Elsie M. Campbell

Helen Storbeck pieced this wall quilt from a beautiful border print to illustrate how different parts of the print, when repeated in the fan blades, create a kaleidoscope effect. I felt that this quilt had an Asian flavor, so I reflected that theme with lotus blossom motifs in the quilting. I so enjoyed working with this quilt that I was inspired to make my own version, *Pharaoh's Phans*.

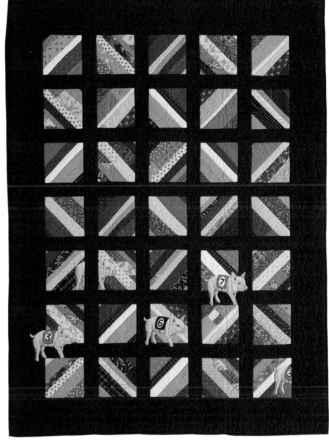

Pigs-in-a-Blanket
44" x 59", 1996

    After collecting pig prints for several months, it was time to construct my *Pigs-in-a-Blanket* quilt. I love making string quilts. I appliquéd pigs from one of my collection of prints *broderie perse* style to the front of the quilt. A simple cable pattern is quilted in the sashing strips, and the outline of the cable is echoed in graduated lines in the outer border. Quilting design can be found on page 95.

Pharaoh's Phans
28" x 60", 1994

    I made my own version of a fan quilt from a beautiful border print. Taking a hint from the striped print, I created a unique quilting pattern for the triangle-shaped parts of this wall quilt. I quilted around printed motifs in the border fabric. Quilting design can be found on page 98.

Serenity
32" x 32", 1990

After joining my first quilt guild, Walnut Valley Quilter's Guild, I participated in a challenge. We started with three specific fabrics and could add up to two more. I created this small wall quilt that is entirely hand pieced and hand quilted. The paisley pattern in

the large ecru portions reflects motifs found in one of the challenge fabrics. This quilt was named the Best of Show and Viewer's Choice winner of the guild challenge and Best of Show at the Kansas State Fair in 1991.

Little Amish Flower Garden
34" x 34", 1995

After reading Carol Doak's first book, *Easy Machine Paper Piecing*, I became fascinated with the paper foundation method for piecing intricate patterns. This quilt was made from a pattern in that book. The borders are quilted with an original continuous undulating feather pattern.

Delicious!
32" x 32", 2000

Appliqué patterns can sometimes become great quilting patterns—and vice versa. In this quilt, the apple motif provided both the appliqué and quilting patterns. I got a little hungry while making this quilt, so I took a bite out of

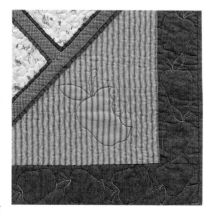

one quilted apple! Smaller versions of the apple were quilted in the borders. By making parts of the apples touch, I was able to machine quilt the border in two passes around the quilt. Quilting designs can be found on page 93.

Spring
21" x 24", 2000

By appliquéing a single motif and framing it with solid color fabrics, I created large open areas for original quilting patterns. The stylized floral motif and butterfly are both surrounded by flowing lines that resemble flower stems and vines, reflecting the mood of the fabric.

A Touch of Blue I
17" x 19", 2001

After quilting my pattern, I decided the quilt needed a touch of color. Bright blue yarn threaded into portions of the design with a trapunto needle created the softened shade of blue. You'll find instructions and the pattern for another version of this miniature masterpiece on page 59.

Christmas Pillow
14" x 14", 2002

I used crayon and colored pencils to add soft, subtle colors to this pillow. The outline pattern on page 105 was first traced in black permanent marker, and then colored. I then quilted the black outlines with black thread.

Tulips Pillow
12" x 12", 1999

Note that several of the single motifs in the corners of the pattern on page 104 were deleted to eliminate stops and starts that are more difficult on machine.

Sweethearts Table Runner

Practice your hand-quilting skills and make a beautiful table runner in the process. A touch of colorful, but easy fusible appliqué and wonderful hand quilting designs create a simple, but very elegant table runner. An embroidered monogram within each heart personalizes this lovely accessory and highlights its classic appeal. When I ran into time constraints while hand quilting this project, my friend Doll Yunker came to the rescue and finished the background quilting.

Quilt Size: 19" x 55"   **Skill Level:** Easy to Intermediate

Materials

- 3½ yards 42"-wide bleached muslin for the quilt top, backing, and binding
- One 6" square each of 3 shades of rose hand-dyed fabric for the flower petals
- One fat quarter (22" x 18") green print for the heart, leaves, and stems
- 24" x 60" piece of batting
- Gold machine or hand embroidery thread for monograms and flower stamens
- Green and rose machine or hand embroidery threads for satin-stitch appliqué
- Green, rose, and white hand-quilting threads
- 18" x 55" piece of freezer paper
- ½ yard lightweight fusible web for appliqué
- Tear-away stabilizer (if doing machine appliqué)

Cutting

Bleached Muslin:

Cut 2 rectangles, 24" x 60" for the top and backing.
Cut 2 strips, 2" x 80" for traditional binding option. (Cut lengthwise from the remaining fabric.)

Appliqué

1. Trace the appliqué patterns on page 58 to the paper side of the fusible web, leaving approximately ½" between motifs. Trace 24 rose petals (F). Trace 2 each of the leaf (B, C, D) and side stem (E) patterns, and 2 of each reversed (BR, CR, DR, ER). You need a total of 12 leaves and 4 side stems. Trace 2 of the end stem (A).

2. Cut the shapes from the fusible web, leaving approximately ¼" around each piece.

3. Fuse the pieces onto the back of the appropriate fabrics according to the manufacturer's instructions. Cut the pieces out exactly on the traced lines. Set aside.

4. Enlarge and trace the quilting patterns on pages 107–108 to make the freezer-paper marking guide as described in Making and Using a Freezer-Paper Marking Guide on page 13.

5. Place the marking guide, dull side up, on the back of the table runner top. Press it in place on the wrong side of the fabric with a hot, dry iron.

6. Turn the table runner right side up. The design lines should shadow through.

7. Position the appliqué pieces on one end of the table runner, aligning them with the design lines on the marking guide. Working with one piece at a time, remove the paper backing and fuse each piece in place, following the manufacturer's recommendations. Repeat for the opposite end of the table runner.

Quilting and Other Stitching

1. Mark the quilting designs, referring to Making and Using a Freezer-Paper Marking Guide on page 13 as needed.

2. Using a see-through ruler as a straight edge, mark the outer straight lines and the straight lines behind the appliqué motifs for background quilting.

3. After you have marked all your quilting lines, remove the marking guide from the table runner.

4. Satin stitch by hand or machine around each appliqué shape. You can also stitch the edges with a hand blanket stitch or buttonhole stitch. If you do machine appliqué, use a tear-away stabilizer underneath the quilt top to ensure smooth stitching and to eliminate puckers.

5. Embroider 2 gold stamens on each flower petal by hand or machine, using a satin stitch.

Embroider stamens by hand or machine.

6. If desired, embroider a monogram letter between the large leaves. You can use machine or hand embroidery, or use a purchased fusible appliqué.

7. Tear away the stabilizer, if used.

Finishing

1. Layer, baste, and quilt the table runner, referring to Stitching up a Storm on page 18 as needed.

2. Block, trim, and square the edges of the table runner and add the binding, using the 2"-wide muslin strips for the binding. Refer to Crossing the Finish Line on page 36 as needed.

Optional Edge Finish

I finished my table runner with a front-to-back finish. There are no binding strips with this method.

1. Trim only the backing and batting ¼" beyond the outermost line of quilting.

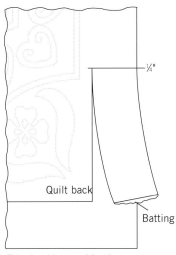

¼"

Quilt back

Batting

Trim backing and batting.

2. Trim the quilt top ½" beyond the trimmed backing and batting (¾" beyond the outermost line of quilting).

3. With the wrong side up, fold the raw edge of the quilt top under ¼".

4. Turn the folded edge over the trimmed edges of the batting and backing and whipstitch it to the backing, as shown.

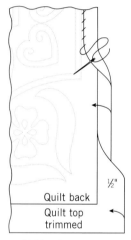

½"

Quilt back

Quilt top trimmed

Fold twice, then whip-stitch.

5. Stitch the folds of the corners securely, and continue whipstitching the top over the backing and batting until you have stitched entirely around the table runner.

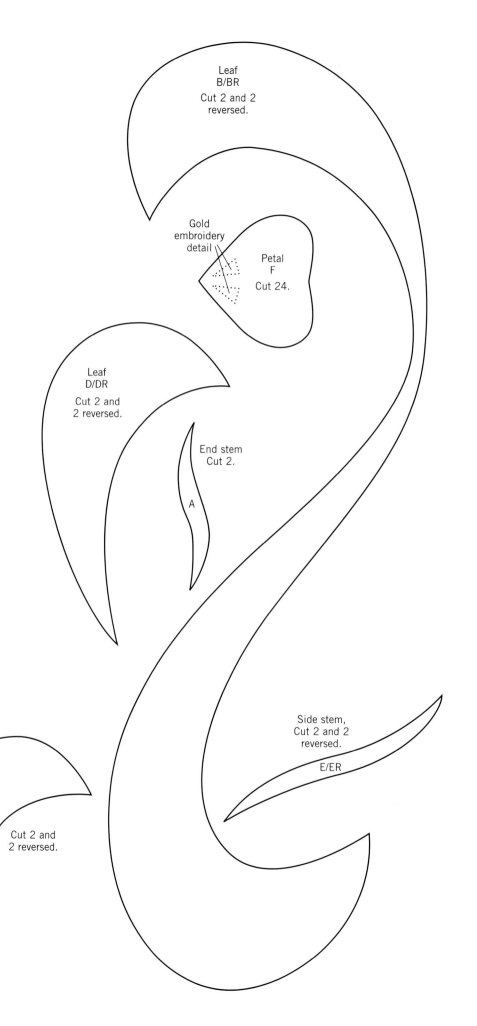

Leaf
B/BR
Cut 2 and 2
reversed.

Gold
embroidery
detail

Petal
F
Cut 24.

Leaf
D/DR
Cut 2 and
2 reversed.

End stem
Cut 2.

A

Side stem,
Cut 2 and 2
reversed.

E/ER

Leaf
C/CR

Cut 2 and
2 reversed.

A Touch of Blue II

Wholecloth quilts present a great opportunity to hand quilt without encountering bulky seams, and the solid color fabric lets your quilting stitches shine without competition from busy prints. Making a minia- ture is a great way to perfect your skills while making something beautiful at the same time. The crowning glory of this diminutive beauty is the trapunto filled with colored yarn. Enjoy stitching this charming little quilt. The quilting design can be found on page 109.

Quilt Size: 14½" x 18"
Skill Level: Intermediate

Materials

- 1⅛ yards bleached muslin for the quilt top, backing, and binding
- 18" x 22" piece of very thin batting*
- 18" x 22" piece of freezer paper
- 1 skein of bright blue 3-ply acrylic yarn
- Trapunto needle

- Crewel embroidery needle or other long, strong needle with a sharp point

*I suggest Thermore™ by Hobbs Fibers, available at most quilt shops.

Cutting

Muslin:

Cut 2 rectangles, 18" x 22" for quilt top and backing.
Cut 2 strips, 1⅛" x 42" for binding.

Marking and Quilting

1. Use the pattern on page 109 to make a freezer-paper marking guide. Refer to Making and Using a Freezer-Paper Marking Guide on page 13 as needed. Mark the quilt top.

2. Using a see-through drafting ruler as a straight edge, mark the crosshatching in the central section and the long, radiating lines.

3. Remove the marking guide from the back of the quilt top.

4. Baste and quilt, referring to Stitching Up a Storm on page 18 as needed.

Adding the Trapunto

1. Thread the trapunto needle with a length of yarn (approximately 36"). Pull the thread through the needle until the ends of the yarn are even. If you have trouble threading the needle, first thread the needle with a double length of quilting thread, cut ends first. Thread the yarn through the loop of quilting thread. Pull the thread loop and gently tug until the yarn is threaded through the eye of the needle. Remove the quilting thread from the yarn loop. Pull one end of the yarn loop completely through the eye of the needle.

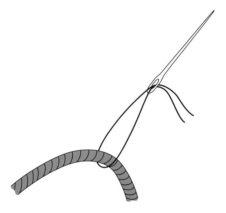

Use a loop of thread to pull the yarn through.

2. Working from the front of the quilt, carefully insert the trapunto needle between the quilt top and batting, extending the needle the full length of the motif to be trapuntoed. Bring the needle out through the surface of the quilt. Take care not to tear any fabric threads either upon entry or exit from the fabric.

Insert the needle through the area to be filled with yarn.

Elsie's Advice

When working with feathers and other tapered motifs, I have found that it is easier to enter the motif at the wide end and exit at the narrow end.

3. Pull the yarn gently through the fabric until the ends of the yarn are nearly even with the surface of the quilt. Holding the scissors flat on the quilt surface, clip the ends slightly beyond the fabric at both the entry and exit points.

Clip the yarn ends.

4. With the point of the crewel needle, work the yarn ends into the filled design area. Manipulate the threads of the weave shut either with the point of the crewel needle or your thumbnail.

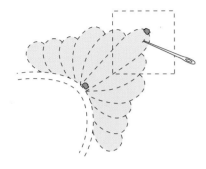

Work yarn ends inside with a needle.

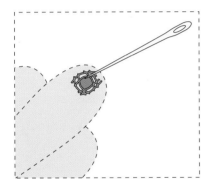

Work the threads together to close the needle hole.

5. Work a second length of doubled yarn into the motif to fill it out, if needed. These yarn lengths should run parallel to the first ones. Continue working until the motif is filled but not distorted.

6. Fill long, narrow channels from one sharp turn in the design to another. It is difficult to bring the needle up in the middle of a channel and manipulate it back into the channel without tearing a large hole in the surface of the fabric. Instead,

try manipulating the fabric onto the needle, scrunching it as needed even around curves. Then bring the needle to the quilt's surface and pull the yarn through the channel. If you found it necessary to scrunch the fabric onto the needle, completely flatten the fabric by gently tugging it back into place before cutting the yarn ends. Work the openings shut.

7. Continue to fill the motifs that you want to appear a pale blue. Refer to the photograph on page 59 to see which areas I filled.

Finishing

Block, trim, and square the edges of the quilt. See Crossing the Finish Line on page 36 as needed.

Single-Fold Binding

Add a single-fold binding to keep the bulk to a minimum on this miniature quilt. Refer to the steps that follow and to Binding on page 38 as needed.

1. Join the two 1⅛" x 42" muslin strips together with a diagonal seam.

2. Press the strip in half lengthwise with right sides together. Open up the binding strip. Fold and press one raw edge in ¼".

3. Pin the open binding strip to the quilt, matching the unfolded edge of the binding with the raw edges of the quilt. Stitch, using a ¼" seam allowance. Miter the corners as you stitch around the quilt.

4. Join the ends of the binding and stitch to the quilt.

5. Fold the binding to the back of the quilt, covering the machine stitching. Blindstitch the folded edge of the binding to the quilt. Form miters at the corners and stitch the miters shut for flat, neat corners.

Quilting Designs

Because hand quilting is my favorite part of the quiltmaking process, I have designed numerous patterns over the years. I've included several here, from miniature designs to feathers and motifs with an international influence.

While writing patterns and articles for *Miniature Quilts* magazine, I began designing a series of quilting patterns for miniature borders and blocks. These were initially used to fill space in the magazine as needed. The patterns became so popular with readers that my designs became a regular feature. If you enjoy making little quilts, I think you'll like the original miniature designs that begin on the next page. Although the border and block patterns are sized to fit tiny masterpieces, they can be enlarged to fit bed-size quilts, too.

Feathers are among my all-time favorite quilting patterns. Traditional and graceful, you'll find them on many fine antique quilts. These flowing motifs are also popular with contemporary quiltmakers. Plain alternate blocks or borders are the perfect place to quilt fancy feather patterns. Feel free to adapt the patterns, beginning on page 69, to your individual quilts. Use them for inspiration or exactly as printed. Just enjoy the process.

When traveling through European countries rich in artistic ethnic traditions, I have always been intrigued with carvings on buildings, motifs on painted cabinetry, and even on delicate eggs, wooden jewelry boxes, and clocks. During my travels, I began to collect small items, and photograph large items and architectural details for quilting pattern ideas. Many of the patterns that begin on page 91 are the result of my travel inspirations.

When I began teaching hand quilting to others, I wanted students to start with patterns on a whole cloth because there would be no seams to interrupt the quilting. I also wanted patterns that were beautiful so students would be inspired to finish the piece. Because straight-line quilting is harder to execute than gentle curves, the patterns feature both kinds of lines; the quilting begins with the curved lines and then progresses to the straight lines with cross-hatching or grids in the plain areas.

The 14" block patterns on pages 101–106 are those I designed for my hand quilting students. These blocks can be used together for a wholecloth quilt, or alone as pillows or wall hangings. Some are suitable for appliqué, or can be colored with crayons or fabric markers before quilting.

I hope you will find a design that is just right for your next quilt, or find inspiration for creating a quilting pattern that is uniquely yours and perfectly suited to your project.

Miniature Quilts
Hearts and Feathers

Fits a 2⅜" border.

Fits a 3⅜" block.

Undulating Feathers

Fits a 1½" border.

Fits a 3½" block.

Ribbons and Feathers

This block is suitable for a memory quilt. The center space is just large enough for a signature written with a fine-line permanent marker.

Fits a 2" border.

Fits a 3" block.

Twirling Leaves

These patterns are also suitable for appliqué.

Fits a 1¼" border.

Fits a 3¼" block.

Forget-Me-Knot

Fits a 1⅞" border.

Fits a 4½" block.

Double Cable

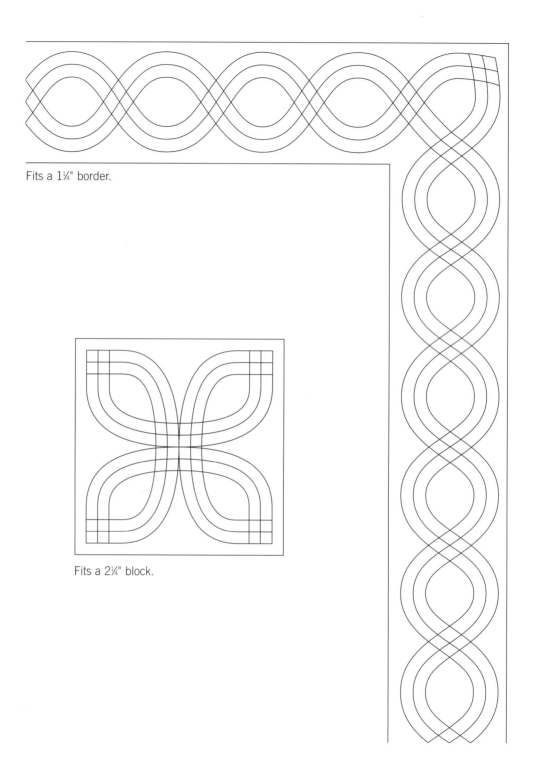

Fits a 1¼" border.

Fits a 2¼" block.

Feather Borders
Straight Feathers with Double Vanes

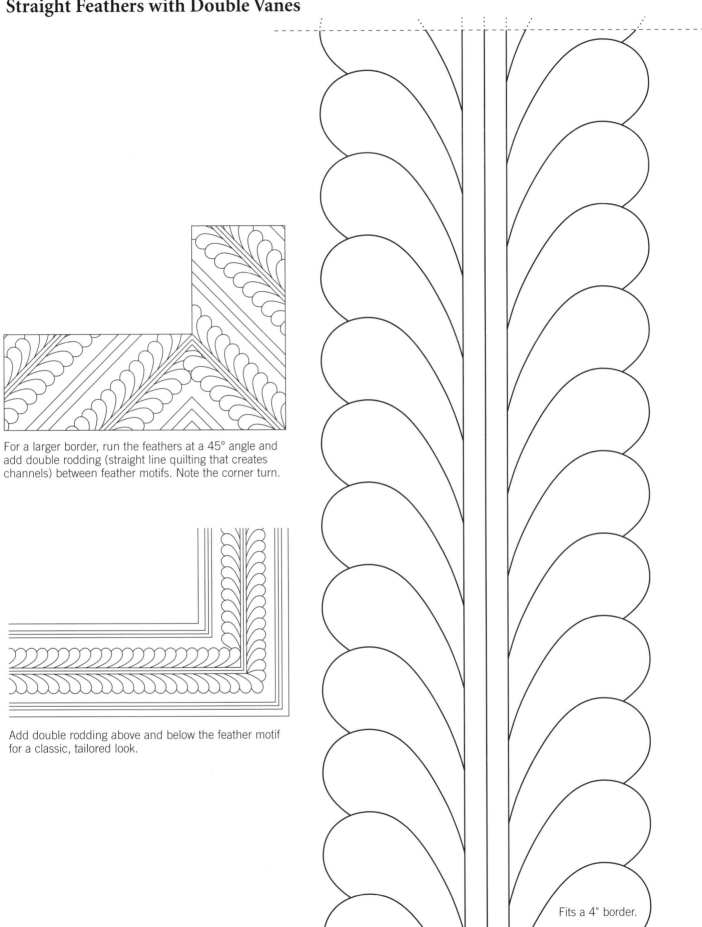

For a larger border, run the feathers at a 45° angle and add double rodding (straight line quilting that creates channels) between feather motifs. Note the corner turn.

Add double rodding above and below the feather motif for a classic, tailored look.

Fits a 4" border.

Cable and Feathers

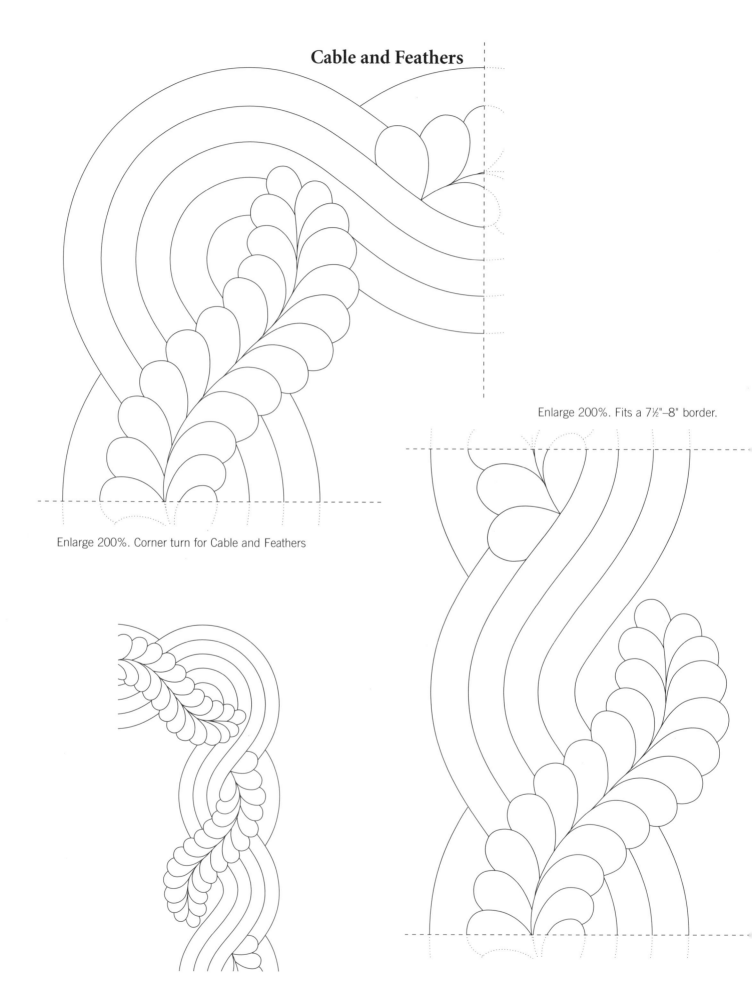

Enlarge 200%. Fits a 7½"–8" border.

Enlarge 200%. Corner turn for Cable and Feathers

Feathered Swag

Enlarge 200%. Corner turn for Feathered Swag

Center

Enlarge 200%. Fits a 4"–4½" border.

Peaches and Cream

The Peaches and Cream designs are interchangeable. Matching lines are provided. The border motifs can end, reverse in the centers of the borders, mirror image from the centers and/or corners, or continue around the border with the feathers all running in the same direction. You decide!

Corner turn for 7" border with almost mirror-imaged design. Note the leaf is just on one side of the center flower.

7" Peaches and Cream Swag End

Match to Corner.

Match to Swag 2.

7" Peaches and Cream Swag 1

Match to Swag 1.

Match to Swag End.

7" Peaches and Cream Swag 2

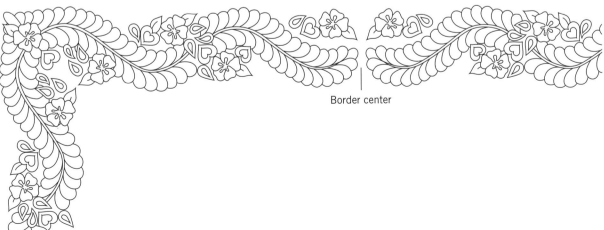

Border center

Match to Swag End.

Match to Center.

7" Peaches and Cream Swag 3

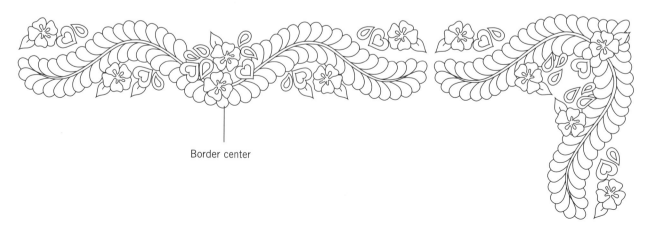

Border center

7" Peaches and Cream Center

4" Peaches and Cream Corner

4" Peaches and Cream Swag, right side

4" Peaches and Cream Swag, left side

Star Flower

The feather border patterns for *Star Flower* (page 51) are given on the following pages. Match the patterns at the lines as indicated for one half of one corner of the border design. Mirror the image at the corner for the complete border.

Enlarge 200%. 13" Star Flower Border Corner
Match at C and D to Section 1.

C/CR   FR   D

Enlarge 200%. 13" Star Flower Border, Section 1
Match at C and D to Corner. Mirror Section 1 and match at CR and FR to Section 2.

Enlarge 200%.
13" Star Flower
Border, Section 2
Match at CR and
FR to mirrored
Section 1. Note:
Rotate this page
180° to match.

FB-06-20-I

Enlarge 110% to fit an 8½"–9" block.

Square Feather

Fits a 7" block.

Hearts and Feather

Fits an 8" block.

Feathered Heart

Fits a 6½" block.

**Tulip Garden
Wedding**

Fits an 8" x 11" area. (See quilt on page 46, where it is used in the corners.)

Tulip Garden Wedding Love Bird

Entire motif fits a 6½" x 12" area. For the complete motif, mirror the image along the dashed line. (See quilt on page 46.)

Large Feathered Heart

Enlarge 200%. Fits a 14" block.

National Emblem Eagle

The following pattern is used in the quilt, *Let Freedom Ring* (page 50). If you choose to use my freezer-paper marking guide technique for marking your quilt, you will need to reverse this image before tracing it, or the eagle will face the opposite direction in your finished quilt.

Enlarge the eagle approximately 228% to fit a 24" corner.

Liberty Bell and Feathers

The following pattern is used in the quilt, *Let Freedom Ring* (page 50). If you choose to use my freezer-paper marking guide technique for marking your quilt, you will need to reverse this image before tracing it, or the crack in the bell will face the opposite direction in your finished quilt.

Fits a 7½" deep triangle.

Other Borders and Blocks
Swiss Border

Enlarge 200%. Fits a 7" border.

Enlarge 200%. Swiss Border Continuation

Czech Border

This pattern reverses direction at the corners and in the center of each border. Repeat the single motif as many times as needed to fill the entire border.

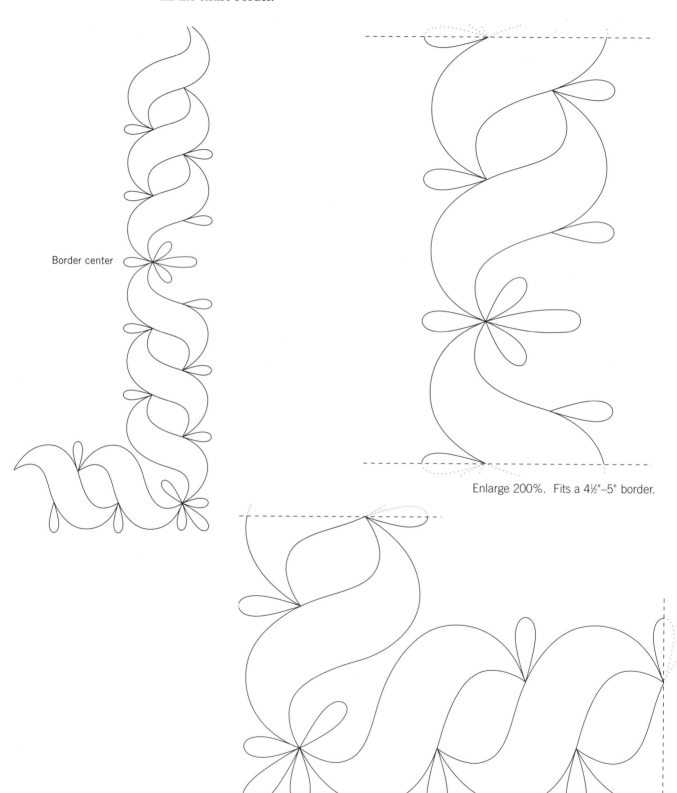

Border center

Enlarge 200%. Fits a 4½"–5" border.

Enlarge 200%. Czech Border Corner

Delicious!

This border and block pattern is suitable for both hand and machine quilting. When machine quilting, complete the pattern in two passes. Refer to page 17 for stitching direction. Repeat the apple motif as many times as needed to fill the border.

Fits a 3½" block. Just for fun, take a bite out of one apple.

Fits a 3½" border.

Acorns and Leaves

Repeat this single motif as many times as needed to fill the border.

Fits a 6" border or a 7½"–8" deep half-square setting triangle.

Double Egg-and-Dart Border

Repeat this single motif as many times as needed to fill the entire border.

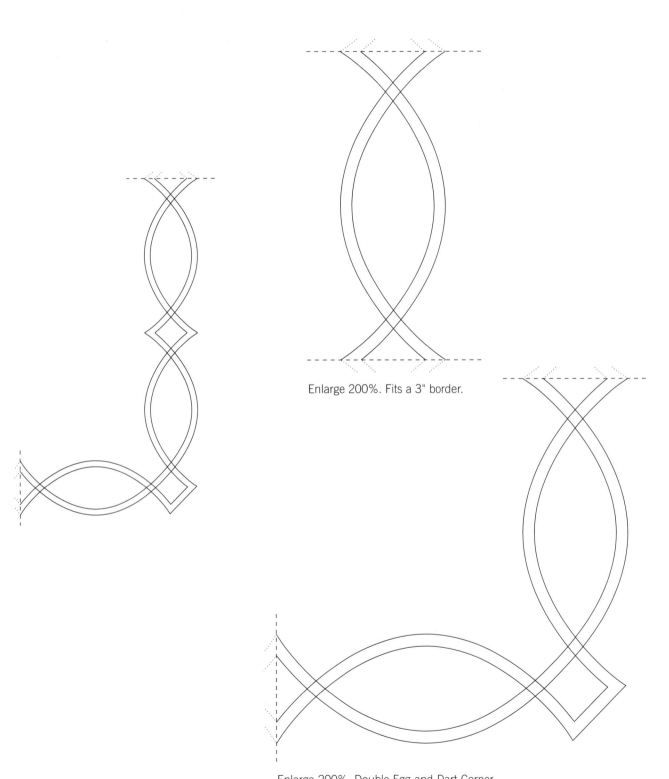

Enlarge 200%. Fits a 3" border.

Enlarge 200%. Double Egg-and-Dart Corner

Russian Border

Repeat this single motif as many times as needed to fill the entire border.

Fits a 6½"–7" border. Mirror the pattern at the dashed lines to make a complete motif.

Russian Block

Fits a 14" block. Join the image along the dashed lines to complete the motif.

Pharoah's Phans

This pattern was designed to fill the open space of fan blocks, but can be completed in a block form by joining the image along dashed lines, as shown. See the quilt on page 53.

Fits a 12" block.

Curly-Cues

This pattern can be mirror-imaged along the dashed lines, or
rotated and repeated for a beautiful block.

Fits a 16" block.

Small Curly-Cues

The large open center of this pattern can be crosshatched, or is
perfect for signatures or other inked designs.

Fits a 15" block. Join image along the dashed lines for the complete motif.

Art Nouveau Butterflies

The large open center of this pattern can be crosshatched.

Fits a 14" block. Join image along the dashed lines to complete the motif.

Floral Wreath

The large open center of this pattern can be quilted with straight diagonal lines.

Fits a 14" block. Join image along the dashed lines to complete the motif.

I Heard It Through the Grapevine

The large open center of the wreath can be crosshatched.

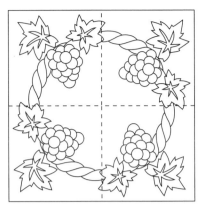

Fits a 14" block. Join image along the dashed lines to complete the motif.

Dutch Tulips

The open centers of the hearts can be crosshatched.

Fits a 14" block. Join image along the dashed lines to complete the motif. Eliminate the corner heart and paisleys to fit a 12" block. See the pillow on page 55.

Christmas Bells

The open center of the wreath can be crosshatched.

Fits a 14" block. Join image along the dashed lines to complete the motif. See the pillow on page 55.

Hummingbird Morning

If you choose to use my Freezer-paper Marking Guide Technique for marking your quilt, you will need to reverse these images before tracing it, or the hummingbird will face the opposite direction in your finished block.

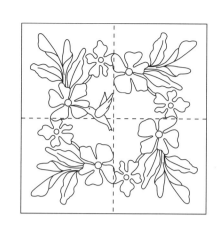

Fits a 14" block. Join image along the dashed lines to complete the motif. Then add the hummingbird motif in one quadrant as indicated by the dotted line.

Projects
Sweethearts Table Runner Part 1

Connect to Part 2.

Enlarge 200%. The total combined design (Part 1 and 2) fits 18" x 54". Mirror the pattern along the center dashed line to complete Part 1.

Sweethearts Table Runner Part 2

Center

Center

Connect to Part 1.

Enlarge 200%. Mirror the pattern along the center dashed lines to complete Part 2.

A Touch of Blue II

Center

A quarter of the design is given here. Mirror the pattern along the center dashed lines to complete the motif.

About the Author

Elsie M. Campbell is an award-winning quilt-maker who travels and teaches across the nation, sharing her unique twist on hand-quilting techniques and quilt design. She grew up in Deer Creek, Oklahoma, as a member of a small General Conference Mennonite community.

Quilts were a part of her everyday life. "I grew up with quilts on every bed. My mother, grandmothers, and aunts all made quilts. They were made to be used and most of them were loved to death. I just thought everyone knew how to quilt," says Elsie.

Elsie graduated from college with a bachelor's degree in Home Economics with an emphasis in clothing and textiles. She taught in public schools until the birth of her first son. A variety of career experiences followed, including that of insurance agent, piano teacher, and custom framer. She then returned to school to earn her master's degree in Special Education. It was during her 13-year career as a special education teacher that Elsie rekindled her love of quilting. Since that time, she has produced many award-winning hand-quilted quilts in addition to constructing many more as gifts for family and friends.

In 1999, Elsie joined the staff of Chitra Publications as a co-editor for *Quilting Today, Traditional Quiltworks* and *Miniature Quilts* magazines. In addition to writing and editing magazine articles, she worked as a freelance writer for Rodale's Successful Quilting Library book series.

For the past three years, Elsie has concentrated her efforts on teaching quiltmaking techniques and writing books and articles from her home in Dodge City, Kansas. Elsie lives with her husband of 32 years, Kenneth Campbell, and their black-and-white tuxedo cat, Jenny. The couple have two sons, Kelly and Kerry, and one daughter-in-law, Hilary.

Elsie is an active member of many different quilt-related organizations. Awards to her credit include First Place finishes in such prestigious shows as the World Quilt and Textile Show, Quilter's Heritage Celebration in Lancaster, Pennsylvania; the International Quilt Festival in Houston, Texas; Sew Near to My Heart Quilt Show in Cincinnati, Ohio; Best of Show at Quilt America! in Indianapolis, Indiana; the Mary Krickbaum Award for Best Hand Quilting from the National Quilt Association; and the American Quilter's Society's Award for Excellence in Hand Workmanship.

Please visit Elsie's website at www.elsiemcampbell.com.

Bibliography

Creating and Selecting Quilting Designs
Cleland, Lee, *Feathers that Fly,* Martingale and Company, Woodinville, WA, 2002.

Cory, Pepper, *Mastering Quilt Marking,* C&T Publishing, Lafayette, CA, 1999.

Crust, Melody and Heather Tewell, *A Fine Line: Techniques and Inspirations for Creating the Quilting Design,* The Quilt Digest Press, a division of McGraw-Hill, New York, NY, 2002.

Dover Publications, Inc.
(Source for copyright-free designs for needleworkers, artists, and craftsmen)
31 East 2nd Street, Mineola, NY 11501
doverpublications.com (Look under the topic Art for Design Library.)

Fritz, Laura Lee, *250 Continuous-Line Quilting Designs for Hand, Machine & Long-Arm Quilters,* C&T Publishing, Lafayette, CA, 2001.

Fritz, Laura Lee, *250 More Continuous-Line Quilting Designs,* C&T Publishing, Lafayette, CA, 2002.

Marston, Gwen and Joe Cunningham, *Quilting with Style: Principles for Great Pattern Design,* American Quilter's Society, Paducah, KY, 1993.

Shackelford, Anita, *Infinite Feathers Quilting Designs,* American Quilter's Society, Paducah, KY, 2002.

Townswick, Jane, Editor, *Choosing Quilting Designs,* Rodale Press, Emmaus, PA, 2001.

Detailed information about:
Batting and Fabric
Hargrave, Harriet, *From Fiber to Fabric,* C&T Publishing, Lafayette, CA, 1997.

Hand Quilting
Anderson, Alex, *Hand Quilting with Alex Anderson,* C&T Publishing, Lafayette, CA, 1998.

Leone, Diana, and Cindy Walter, *Fine Hand Quilting, 2nd Edition,* Krause Publications, Iola, WI, 2000.

McElroy, Roxanne, *That Perfect Stitch: The Secrets of Fine Hand Quilting,* The Quilt Digest Press, a Division of McGraw-Hill, New York, NY, 1997.

Morris, Patricia J., *Perfecting the Quilting Stitch: The Ins & Outs,* American Quilter's Society, Paducah, KY, 2001.

Rodale Quilt Book Editors, *Flawless Hand Quilting,* Rodale Press, Emmaus, PA, 1999.

Simms, Ami, *How to Improve Your Quilting Stitch,* Mallery Press, Flint, MI, 1987.

Machine Quilting
Fanning, Robbie and Tony, *The Complete Book of Machine Quilting,* Chilton Book Company, Radnor, PA, 1994.

Gaudynski, Diane, *Guide to Machine Quilting,* American Quilter's Society, Paducah, KY, 2002.

Hargrave, Harriet, *Heirloom Machine Quilting: A Comprehensive Guide to Hand-Quilted Effects Using Your Sewing Machine, 3rd ed.,* C&T Publishing, Lafayette, CA, 1995.

Soltys, Karen Costello, Editor, *Fast & Fun Machine Quilting,* Rodale Press, Emmaus, PA, 1997.

Townswick, Jane, Editor, *Easy Machine Quilting.* Rodale Press, Emmaus, PA, 1996.

Quilt Competition Guidelines
Morris, Patricia J., *The Judge's Task: How Award-Winning Quilts Are Selected,* American Quilter's Society, Paducah, KY, 1993.

Resources

Hand-Dyed Fabrics
Cherrywood Fabrics; P.O. Box 486, Brainerd, MN 56401; (888) 298-0967; www.cherrywoodfabrics.com

Fabrics to Dye For; Two Rivers Road, Pawacatuck, CT 06379; (888) 322-1319; www.fabricstodyefor.com

Primrose Gradations; P.O. Box 6, Two Harbors, MN 55616; (888) 393-2787; www.dyearts.com/store/commerce.cgi

Ricky Tims Art Quilt Studio; 6043 Newcombe; Arvada, CO 80004; (303) 736-4801; www.rickytims.com

Marking Pencils, Thimbles, Rulers, and Other Notions
Clotilde, LLC, P.O. Box 7500, Big Sandy, TX 75755-7500; (800) 772-2891; www.clotilde.com (General sewing and quilting supplies)

Clover Needlecraft, Inc., 1007 E. Cominguez St., Suite L, Carson, CA 90746; (800) 233-1703; www.clover-usa.com (Erasable fabric marking pens and pencils, thimbles, needles, and other notions)

Prym-Dritz Corporation, P.O. Box 5028, Spartanburg, SC 29304; (800) 255-7796; www.dritz.com (W. H. Collins Nonce white marking pencils)

Heartland Quiltworks, Box 10, Bow Island, Alberta T0K 0G0; (888) 867-9175; www.heartlandquiltworks.ca (Compact floor and lap quilting hoops and frames)

Entaco Limited, Royal Victoria Works, Birmingham Road, Studley, Warwickshire, B80 7AP England; +44 (0) 1527 852306; www.entaco.com (John James quilting needles, trapunto needles, long darners for basting, and magnetic-top thimbles)

Nancy's Notions, 333 Beichl Ave., Beaver Dam, WI 53916-0683; (800) 833-0690; www.nancys-notions.com (General sewing and quilting supplies)

Miscellaneous
Bear Thread Designs, P.O. Box 11452, Highland, TX 77562; (281) 462-0661; www.bearthreaddesigns.com (Sew-Clean all natural fabric spot and stain remover)

Gloves in a Bottle, Inc.; P.O. Box 615; Montrose, CA 91021; (800) 600-1881; www.glovesinabottle.com (Gloves in a Bottle Dry Skin Protectorant)

Sailor Pen Corporation, 121 Bethea Road, Suite 307, Fayetteville, GA 30214; (800) 248-4583; www.sailorpen.com (Distributors of Sailor® Leafits tacky dots)

Pieces Be With You; Susan Cleveland, 54336 237th Ave.; West Concord, MN 55985; www.piecesbewithyou.com (Piping Hot Binding Trimming Tool)

Orvus® WA Paste, product of The Procter & Gamble Company. Ask for it at your local quilt shop or farm supply store.

Quilter's Rule International, LLC; 817 Mohr Ave., Waterford, WI 53185; (800) 343-8671; www.quiltersrule.com (Marking Pencil Removal for Hobby, Crafts, Sewing and Quilting)

For the Star Flower pattern (available Fall, 2004) and other fine books, ask for a free catalog:
C&T Publishing, Inc.
P.O. Box 1456
Lafayette, CA 94549
(800) 284-1114
Email: ctinfo@ctpub.com
Website: www.ctpub.com

Quilting Supplies
Cotton Patch Mail Order, 3405 Hall Lane, Dept.CTB, Lafayette, CA 94549; (800) 835-4418; (925) 283-7883; Email: quiltusa@yahoo.com; Website: www.quiltusa.com

Note: Fabrics used in the quilts shown may not be currently available because fabric manufacturers keep most fabrics in print for only a short time.

Quilt Shows
Check with these organizations or their websites for exact show dates. For local and regional shows, check with local and area quilt guilds and shops and/or look in quilting magazines.

American Quilters Society (2 shows: Paducah, KY, and Nashville, TN), P.O. Box 3290, Paducah, KY 42002-3290; (270) 898-7903; www.aqsquilt.com

International Quilt Association (3 shows: Quilts: A World of Beauty—Houston, TX, IQA Spring Show—Chicago, Quilt Expo—Europe), 7660 Woodway Drive, Suite 550, Houston, TX 77063; (713) 781-6864; iqa@quilts.com; www.quilts.org/IQA

David M. and Peter J. Mancuso, Inc. (5 shows: World Quilt and Textile Show (in various locations); Pennsylvania National Quilt Extravaganza in Ft. Washington, PA; Pacific International Quilt Show in Santa Clara, CA; Williamsburg Quilt Festival in Williamsburg, VA; and the Quilt and Sewing Fest at Myrtle Beach, SC), P.O. Box 667, New Hope, PA 18938; www.quiltfest.com

Index

Note: References in *italic* are quilt photographs.